TOP 10
ORLANDO

RICHARD GRULA
JIM & CYNTHIA TUNSTALL

EYEWITNESS TRAVEL

Left **Mennello Museum** Center **Drag queen diva** Right **Merritt Island National Wildlife Refuge**

LONDON, NEW YORK,
MELBOURNE, MUNICH AND DELHI
www.dk.com

Produced by Departure Lounge, London
Reproduced by Colourscan, Singapore
Printed and bound by South China Printing Co. Ltd
First American Edition, 2002
10 11 12 13 10 9 8 7 6 5 4 3 2 1

Published in the United States by DK Publishing,
375 Hudson Street, New York, New York 10014

**Reprinted with revisions
2004, 2006, 2008, 2010
Copyright 2002, 2010
© Dorling Kindersley Limited**

Published in Great Britain by
Dorling Kindersley Limited.

A catalog record for this book is available from
the Library of congress.

ISSN 1479 344X
ISBN 978-0-75666-176-2

Within each Top 10 list in this book, no
hierarchy of quality or popularity is
implied. All 10 are, in the editor's
opinion, of roughly equal merit.

MIX
Paper from
responsible sources
FSC™ C018179

Contents

Orlando's Top 10

The information in this DK Eyewitness Top 10 Travel Guide is checked regularly.
Every effort has been made to ensure that this book is as up-to-date as possible at the time of
going to press. Some details, however, such as telephone numbers, opening hours, prices,
gallery hanging arrangements and travel information are liable to change. The publishers
cannot accept responsibility for any consequences arising from the use of this book, nor for
any material on third party websites, and cannot guarantee that any website address in this
book will be a suitable source of travel information. We value the views and suggestions of
our readers very highly. Please write to: Publisher, DK Eyewitness Travel Guides,
Dorling Kindersley, 80 Strand, London, Great Britain WC2R 0RL.

Left **Believe show at SeaWorld** Center **Universal Studios** Right **Gatorland**

Left **SeaWorld Orlando** Right **Kennedy Space Center**

Key to abbreviations
Adm *admission charge payable* **DA** *disabled access*

3

ORLANDO
TOP 10

ORLANDO'S TOP 10

TOP 10 Orlando's Highlights

One word describes Orlando's transformation in the last three decades: stunning. The city and its suburbs have gone through a Cinderella-like metamorphosis, where plain Jane has become a worldly beauty. Millions of tourists are seduced every year by sophisticated resorts, a wide range of theme parks, must-see attractions, happening nightclubs, and winning restaurants. Here are the Top 10 Orlando sights – Orlando's best of the best.

1 The Magic Kingdom Park
The park that started Disney's Florida empire combines fantasy, adventure, and the future in a package of rides and shows that focuses on Disney movies and TV programs. *See pp8–11.*

2 Epcot
Inquiring minds love this Disney park, which features technology in Future World and the culture, architecture and enticing food of 11 nations in World Showcase. *See pp12–15.*

3 Disney Hollywood Studios
Lights, camera, action! Movies, TV shows and stomach-churning thrill rides come together in a theme park that sometimes also serves as a working studio. *See pp16–17.*

4 Disney's Animal Kingdom Park
Visitors are brought face to face with the wild world of animals, but this kingdom's spacious environmental design doesn't always offer a front-row seat. *See pp18–19.*

5 Islands of Adventure
Universal's top-of-the-pile theme park is a magnet for thrill jockeys, with some of the fastest, highest, and best rides in town. Be warned that 9 of its 13 rides have height or health restrictions, so it's not for the young, weak of stomach, or squeamish. *See pp20–23.*

Previous pages **Incredible Hulk Ride, Islands of Adventure**

Universal Studios Florida

What Disney can do, Universal can equal. The movie and TV themes here can make people's wildest dreams come true or worst nightmares a (special effects) reality. From Jaws to Terminator, the silver screen comes to life. *See pp24–7.*

SeaWorld Orlando

Its laid-back pace, educational angle, and animal actors make this a popular stop for those wanting a break from the lines and stifling crowds at other parks. *See pp28–31.*

Wet 'n Wild

Some say it's hard to beat Disney's water parks, but this rival has the most thrills money can buy on the city's water scene. *See pp34–5.*

Merritt Island

Located at the Kennedy Space Center, this wildlife refuge is great for learning about local and migrating animals, while also enjoying a bit of fishing or hiking. *See pp36–7.*

Kennedy Space Center

The appeal of man in space has turned America's No. 1 space center into a stellar attraction complete with live shuttle and rocket launches. *See pp38–41.*

Orlando's Top 10

For more on the Top 10 sights in Orlando **See pp42–85**

7

🔟 The Magic Kingdom® Park

Walt Disney's first Florida theme park opened in 1971, envisaged as a place where dreams could come true, even if only for a little while. It took six years and $400 million to create "Disneyland East," which has surpassed Walt's own dream: instead of being a spin-off of California's Disneyland Park, it has become the USA's most popular theme park, attracting more than 15 million visitors every year (some 40,000 each day). Although little has changed in 30 years, with more than 40 major attractions and countless minor ones, this is a true fantasy land for the young and young at heart.

🦃 A smoked turkey leg at Tomorrowland's Lunching Pad makes a good quick bite, but it's cheaper to bring your own snacks and water (bottles can be filled at the park's numerous fountains).

🎢 FastPass *(see p132)* cuts the amount of time spent standing in line for the park's most popular rides and shows.

The little publicized E Ride Nights let 5,000 people into the park at a reduced rate for three hours on select nights.

Consider visiting midweek, as the park is at its busiest on weekends and early in the week.

As in all Disney parks, smoking is only allowed in designated outside areas.

🌐 World Drive • Map F1
• 407-824-4321 • www.disneyworld.com • Open at least 9am–7pm daily, call for seasonal hours.
• Adm (1-day ticket): adults $79, children (3–9) $68 (including tax). Children under 3 go free.

Top 10 Attractions

1. Splash Mountain
2. Big Thunder Mountain Railroad
3. The Barnstormer at Goofy's Wiseacre Farm
4. Space Mountain
5. Stich's Great Escape
6. Buzz Lightyear's Space Ranger Spin
7. The Many Adventures of Winnie the Pooh
8. Cinderella's Golden Carrousel
9. The Magic Carpets of Aladdin
10. Pirates of the Caribbean

Splash Mountain
Disney's 1946 film *Song of the South* inspires this wildly popular flume ride, with Brer Rabbit leading the way through swamps, caves, and "the Laughing Place." Expect twists, turns, and a 52-ft (16-m), 45-degree, 40-mph (64-kmph) climax.

Big Thunder Mountain Railroad
Not the raciest of coasters, but the turns and dips, and realistic scenery, combine to make this an exciting trip on a runaway train through gold-rush country *(above)*.

The Barnstormer at Goofy's Wiseacre Farm
Kids and some parents love this mini-roller coaster, which looks like a crop duster plane with Goofy at the controls.

Space Mountain
Orlando's first in-the-dark roller coaster is a ride on a rocket that shoots through hairpin turns and drops at what feels like breakneck speed, although top speed is only 28 mph (45 kmph). The cosmic effects and detail enhance this thrilling ride.

Stitch's Great Escape
This family-friendly adventure is based on the mayhem of Stitch's experiment in outer space. The ride uses sophisticated technology, with sights, sounds, and smells to add to the pandemonium.

6 Buzz Lightyear's Space Ranger Spin

Use the laser cannons on the dashboard to set off sight-and-sound effects as you hurtle through the sky and help *Toy Story's* most famous hero save the world.

7 The Many Adventures of Winnie the Pooh

Pooh, Eeyore, and a whole host of A. A. Milne's lovable characters come to life in this tranquil ride through the Hundred Acre Wood.

Magic Kingdom Park Plan

8 Cinderella's Golden Carrousel

This wonderfully refurbished 1917 carousel is a real beauty. It has handsome wooden horses and an organ that plays Disney classics. Kids love it, and adults love reminiscing about the rides of yesteryear.

Park Guide

Due to the crowds and distance involved, it takes around 20 minutes to get from the parking lots (via tram, boat, or monorail) to the park's attractions. Once inside, the Tip Board at the end of Main Street USA has the latest information on the length of lines and times of shows. Park maps are available from Guest Services to the left of the entrance. You'll need at least a day or parts of several to get the most out of the Magic Kingdom.

9 The Magic Carpets of Aladdin

This Disney ride has four-passenger carpets which glide gently up and down and from side to side around a giant genie's bottle. But watch out for the sneaky, water-spitting camels.

10 Pirates of the Caribbean

Timbers are a-shiver as your boat cruises past a town under siege from a band of rum-soaked, Audio-Animatronic buccaneers. Dank dungeons, yo-ho-ho's, and brazen wenches – all scurvy pirate life is here.

Attraction number		1	2	3	4	5	6	7	8	9	10
Minimum height:	(inches)	40	40	35	44	–	–	–	–	–	–
	(cm)	102	102	89	112	–	–	–	–	–	–
Recommended age group		8+	9+	4+	9+	9+	all	all	all	3+	3+
Duration (minutes)		10	4	1	3	15	5	4	2	3	8

For information on Disney's tour options See p129

Cinderella Castle with Wishes Nighttime Spectacular

🔟 Shows & Next Best Rides

1 Wishes Nighttime Spectacular
This explosive show runs nightly during summer and holidays (occasionally at other times the year). Liberty Square, Mickey's Toontown Fair, and Frontierland are the best areas in the park to take in the fabulous display. If you want to view from outside the Magic Kingdom, Disney's Grand Floridian, Polynesian, Contemporary, and Wilderness Lodge resorts all have good views from upper floors.

2 Walt Disney World Railroad
The antique steam-driven trains that travel this 1.5-mile (2-km) perimeter track offer a good overview of the park's sights, but more importantly allow you to get from A to B without the legwork. It stops at City Hall, Main Street USA, Frontierland, and Mickey's Toontown Fair.

3 Cinderella Castle
Standing 185 ft (56 m) high, this park icon is a sight to behold. Complete with Gothic spires, it's the quintessential fairytale castle, reminiscent of Neuschwanstein, mad King Ludwig of Bavaria's creation. Inside, there's only one thing of interest to visitors, the Cinderella's Royal Table restaurant, where guests can partake of a character breakfast (see p71).

4 Snow White's Scary Adventures
This ride lost some of its scary scenes with the evil queen and wicked witch to make it more enjoyable for smaller children. The queen still makes an appearance but is now joined by good-girl Snow White and the Prince.

5 It's a Small World
The insidious theme song will eat at your brain for months

after you visit, but small kids adore this slow-boat cruise through "lands" where small, Audio-Animatronic, costumed characters sing *It's a Small World After All* in their Munchkin-like voices.

Hall of Presidents
Every US president has an Audio-Animatronic likeness in this fascinating educational show that really highlights the wizardry of Walt Disney Imagineers (designers). The presidents nod and wave, and Abe Lincoln is the keynote speaker.

Mickey's PhilharMagic
Disney magic meets Disney music in a 3-D film spectacular starring Mickey Mouse, Donald Duck, and other favorite Disney characters animated in a way never seen before. Set in the PhilharMagic concert hall in Fantasyland.

Haunted Mansion
A corny yet fun special-effects show with a cult following. It's a slow-moving, slightly scary ride-in-the-dark that passes a ghostly ball, graveyard band, and weird flying objects.

Mickey's Toontown Fair
Bring your autograph books to Mickey's Toontown Fair – inside the fairground's candy-striped tents are many Disney characters. There's lots of fun for little kids, such as spongy Toon Park, with its foam topiary animals.

Magic Kingdom Park Plan

Country Bear Jamboree
Audio-Animatronic bears croon and bellow songs in this knee-slapping revue. The finale has the audience hooting and clapping for an encore.

Magic Kingdom Parades
During summer (and occasionally at other times of the year) a key park event is the evening parade (times vary). The original show was the Main Street Electrical Parade, which was christened at California's Disneyland Park before moving to the Magic Kingdom in 1977. Its replacement is the bigger, better, and brighter SpectroMagic. This electrifying, 20-minute extravaganza brings fountains, creatures, and floats filled with Disney characters to "light". It has no less than 204 speakers cranking out 72,000 watts, uses 75 tons of batteries (enough to power 90 houses for the duration), and 100 miles (160 km) of fiber-optic cable. The whole show is powered by 30 mini-computers. Arrive early and try to find a spot in front of the castle. If you can't stay until dark falls, there's a 15-minute Share the Dream Come True Parade (3pm daily) where guests can see their favorite Disney characters in a procession that leaves from Frontierland to finish off down Main Street USA.

Orlando's Top 10

Attraction number	1	2	3	4	5	6	7	8	9	10
Recommended age group	all	all	all	3+	3+	8+	all	8+	3–10	all
Duration (minutes)	20	20	–	3	11	30	15	8	–	17

TOP 10 Epcot®

Walt Disney imagined Epcot (Experimental Prototype Community of Tomorrow) as a futuristic township where people could live, work, and play in technologically enhanced splendor. After his death in 1966, the idea changed dramatically, and Epcot opened in 1982 as a park of two halves: Future World focuses on science, technology, and the environment, while World Showcase spotlights the cultures of several nations. The pairing works because both sections are educational and appeal to curious adults and kids alike. Be warned, the park is vast, a fact that has led some to joke that its name is an acronym for "Every Person Comes Out Tired."

Future World: the Coral Reef in the Living Seas Pavilion is way better than most in-park restaurants *(see p95)*. Book ahead. World Showcase: Try fresh pastries at the Patisserie in the French Pavilion.

Use FastPass *(see p132)* a ride reservation system.

Save time and energy by using the shuttle boats to cross from Future World to the World Showcase.

This theme park is best toured in two days, if not more.

⊗ Epcot Center Dr, Walt Disney World Resort
• Map G2
• 407-824-1911
• www.disneyworld.com
• Future World: Opens 10am–7pm daily; World Showcase: Opens 11am–9pm daily. Hours are often extended during holidays and in summer months.
• Adm: adults $79, children (3–9) $68 (including tax). Children under 3 go free.

Top 10 Future World Exhibits

1. Test Track
2. Innoventions East
3. Innoventions West
4. The Seas with Nemo & Friends
5. Ellen's Energy Adventure
6. Honey, I Shrunk the Audience
7. Soarin
8. Mission: SPACE
9. Spaceship Earth
10. Living with the Land

Test Track

This ride takes you through the tests carried out on automobile prototypes before they hit the consumer market. Riders get to experience brake tests, S-curves, and a 12-second, 65-mph (104-kmph) burst of speed. You must be at least 40 inches (102 cm) tall.

Innoventions East

A refrigerator that can compile a grocery list and a toilet seat with a built-in warmer are among the "smart" furnishings in the House of Innoventions exhibit. Kids like this pavilion's Internet Zone with games such as virtual tag.

Innoventions West

Few can resist Video Games of Tomorrow, a Sega presentation that lets visitors try out next generation games. In the same pavilion, Medicine's New Vision is an exhibit that offers video games along a medical theme.

The Seas with Nemo & Friends

Board a "clamobile" and join your undersea pals to find Nemo. In the same pavilion is the interactive show "Turtle Talk with Crush," also inspired by the same Pixar film.

Ellen's Energy Adventure

A show-and-ride focusing on themes from "fossil fuel" dinosaurs to future energy concerns.

For more on Walt Disney World Resort attractions See pp88–91

Honey I Shrunk the Audience

Get ready to flinch during the Imagination Pavilion's larger-than-life film show. Seats vibrate as you're terrorized by giant mice. The family cat and dog, and a colossal 5-year-old also loom large before you "escape."

Soarin

Feel the exhilarating rush of this free-flying hang-gliding adventure over the magnificent landscapes of California. You must be at least 40 inches (102 cm) tall to take this ride.

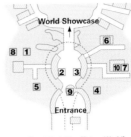

Epcot Park Plan (Future World)

Mission: SPACE

This popular thrill ride takes you on a journey to space with a crash landing on Mars. It is intense and not for anyone prone to motion sickness, or sensitive to tight spaces, loud noises or spinning. If you don't go on the "Mission" you can enjoy interactive games at the "Advance Training Lab."

Park Guide

The main entrance is convenient for Future World, where nine pavilions encircle Spaceship Earth. Getting to World Showcase Lagoon and the 11 nations beyond requires a longer trek, though handy boat shuttles run from Showcase Plaza to the pavilions of Germany and Morocco. A second entrance, at International Gateway, is accessible from Disney's Yacht Club, Beach Club, and BoardWalk Inn resorts. Maps that give up-to-date information are available at both entrances.

Spaceship Earth

The ride inside is nothing to write home about. But, this giant golf ball – actually a 180-ft (55-m) geosphere *(above)* – is an engineering marvel, made of 11,324 triangular aluminum panels that absorb the rain rather than letting it run off.

Living with the Land

The best of the vast Land Pavilion's exhibits involves a boat ride through rain forest, desert, and prairie biomes. It's followed by a look at agricultural experiments including hydroponics and growing plants in simulated Martian soil.

Attraction number	1	2	3	4	5	6	7	8	9	10
Recommended age group	8+	8+	8+	all	all	all	8+	12+	all	all
Duration (minutes)	5	–	–	30	32	9	5	45	17	13

For science on a smaller scale at the Orlando Science Center **See p60 & p113**

Norway Pavilion

TOP10 World Showcase Pavilions

Canada
1 The star attraction here is the inspirational 360-degree CircleVision film, *O Canada!*, which reveals some of the country's scenic wonders. You also get to experience traveling by dogsled. Outside, Canada's rugged terrain is convincingly re-created. Gardens that are based on Victoria's Butchart gardens, a replica of an Indian village, and the Northwest Mercantile store, selling items such as tribal crafts and Canadian maple syrup, can be explored.

China
2 The CircleVision movie, *Reflections of China*, is a fascinating journey through China's natural and man-made riches. The pavilion features a 15th-century Ming dynasty temple, a ceremonial gate, and tranquil gardens. The Yong Feng Shangdian Department Store *(see p92)* is a wonderful treasure trove of Asian goodies. Try not to miss the dynamic Dragon Legend Acrobats who perform several times each day.

Morocco
3 Look for the Koutoubia minaret, a copy of the tower from a 12th-century mosque in Marrakesh, and you've found this exotic pavilion. Inside, the typical souk architecture is embellished by beautiful carvings and mosaics. The Casbah marketplace *(see p92)* is bursting with hard-to-resist crafts sold by "merchants," and you can see carpets being woven on looms. "Local" cuisine such as couscous is available in the Pavilion's restaurant *(see p95)*.

American Adventure
4 Enhance your knowledge of US history in a 30-minute dramatization featuring Audio-Animatronic actors. Mark Twain and Benjamin Franklin are the narrators who explain key events, including the

writing of the Declaration of Independence, and Susan B. Anthony speaks out for women's rights. The Voices of Liberty singers perform in the main hall of the pavilion, which is modeled on Philadelphia's Liberty Hall.

Japan

A breathtaking five-story pagoda, based on Nara's 8th-century Horyuji temple, forms the centerpiece of this architecturally amazing pavilion. The traditional Japanese gardens are pretty impressive, too, and a perfect spot to escape the throngs. The peace and quiet is only occasionally broken by the beat of drums: go investigate: the Matsuriza troupe is one of the best shows in Epcot.

Norway

Norway's Maelstrom ride takes you on a 10-minute journey through fiords and fairy-tale forests in a dragon-headed vessel. You land in a 10th-century Viking village, where a short film portrays Norway's natural treasures. The realistic replica of Oslo's 14th-century Akershus Castle houses the restaurant (see p95).

United Kingdom

Examples of typical British architecture through the ages line the quaint cobblestone streets here. Apart from shops selling quintessential British merchandise

IllumiNations

Created to celebrate the millennium, Epcot's stunning fireworks and laser show is still thrilling visitors every night at 9pm. It is a grand half-hour, sound-and-vision nightcap which also brings the World Showcase Lagoon fountains into the act. There are scores of good viewing places all around the edge of the Lagoon.

Future World

Epcot Park Plan (World Showcase)

(teas, china, crystal, and more), there's also a park with a bandstand and Beatles impersonators providing entertainment.

Mexico

El Rio del Tiempo (River of Time) is an eight-minute multimedia boat ride that explores Mexico's past and present, from the Yucatan's Mayan pyramids (the pavilion is housed in a replica of one) to the urban bustle of Mexico City life. Mariachis entertain, and there's a *plaza* with stalls selling colorful souvenirs such as sombreros, *piñatas*, and leather goods.

France

This pavilion sports scale replicas, including the Eiffel Tower, and shops selling French products. The 18-minute, five-screen film, which sweeps through glorious landscapes accompanied by the music of French composers is a highlight.

Germany

In this cartoon-like, archetypal German village, you'll find a miniature model railroad, including a wonderfully detailed Bavarian Village. The Biergarten restaurant (complete with brass band) serves traditional food, and shops sell everything from Hummel figurines to wines and cuckoo clocks.

Disney Hollywood Studios

Like Universal Studios, Disney Hollywood Studios underscores Orlando's standing as a small, but growing, film production center and offers an up-close look at the world of "Lights! Camera! Action!". The park cost $300 million to create and the result is an effective fusion of fun and information; the attractions tend to be complex, involving rides, shows, and educational commentary, so there really is something for everyone. Nostalgic references to Hollywood's heyday are balanced by high-tech trickery, making this a must for anyone with even a remote interest in the movies.

A hand-dipped ice-cream cone at Hollywood Scoops slides down a treat, but for more substantial refreshment, try the Sci-Fi Dine-In Theater, serving diner fare in a 1950s retro setting, where guests can watch B-movie clips.

Use FastPass *(see p132),* a ride reservation system, to cut the amount of time spent standing in line for the most popular rides and shows.

As in all Disney parks, smoking is only allowed in designated outdoor areas.

The Magic of Disney Animation is a tour that takes you behind the Fantasmic! scenes and lets you try your hand at painting an animation cel. Call 407-939-8687.

- Epcot Resorts Blvd
- Map G2
- 407-824-4321
- www.disneyworld.com
- Open at least 9am–7pm, sometimes later
- Adm: adults $79, children (3–9) $68 (including tax), children under 3 go free.

Top 10 Attractions

1. Rock 'n' Roller Coaster Starring Aerosmith
2. Twilight Zone™ Tower of Terror
3. Fantasmic!
4. Indiana Jones™ Epic Stunt Spectacular
5. Muppet™Vision 3-D
6. Disney Hollywood Studios Backlot Tour
7. Journey into Narnia: Creating The Lion, The Witch and The Wardrobe
8. Star Tours
9. Beauty and the Beast Live on Stage
10. Voyage of the Little Mermaid

1 Rock 'n' Roller Coaster Starring Aerosmith
A sign warns, "prepare to merge as you've never merged before," but by then it's far too late. Your limo zooms from 0 to 60 mph (97 kmph) in 2.8 seconds and into multiple inversions as Aerosmith blares at 32,000 watts *(above).*

2 Twilight Zone™ Tower of Terror
The spooky surroundings are a façade in front of the real terror, a gut-tightening, 13-story fall. To many, it's Disney's best thrill ride.

4 Indiana Jones™ Epic Stunt Spectacular
Indy's action-packed day is full of thrills and spills, and near-death encounters. A stunt co-ordinator explains how it's all done.

5 Muppet™Vision 3-D
Miss Piggy, Kermit, and the rest of the crew star in a show celebrating both Henson's legacy and Disney's special-effects wizardry and audio-animatronics.

3 Fantasmic!
Lasers, fireworks, waterborne images, and a sorcerer mouse are the stars of this end-of-day extravaganza that pits the forces of good against Disney villains such as Cruella De Ville and Maleficent. Performance times vary seasonally.

For another movie-flavored theme park See pp24–7

Disney Hollywood Studios Backlot Tour

What begins as a tram tour through movie sets and the prop department ends at Catastrophe Canyon. Here, explosions, floods, and fire give riders a bit of a shake-up before getting to see behind the Canyon's scenes.

Journey into Narnia: Creating The Lion, The Witch and The Wardrobe

Enter the wardrobe and find yourself in the wintry forest on the other side. Continuous 15-minute walking tours explain how this spectacular film was made. Also on view are elaborate costumes and many props.

Entrance

Disney Hollywood Studios Park Plan

Star Tours

Climb in and swallow hard: your 40-seat spacecraft is going on a journey riddled with dips, bumps, and laser fire. The ride's technology may be a bit outdated, but forgiving Star Wars fans still say this ride hits the spot.

Park Guide

Pick up a map from Guest Services, to the left of the entrance. Staff are on hand to help you find your way around and provide information. The tip board at Sunset and Hollywood boulevards lists up-to-the-minute information on show schedules, wait times, visiting celebrities, and ride or show closures. This park tends to be less busy at the beginning of the week, when many visitors hit the Magic Kingdom or Epcot, and it can easily be tackled in one day.

Beauty and the Beast Live on Stage!

The music from the animated film alone is enough to sell this Broadway-style show. The sets, costumes, and production numbers are pretty spectacular, too.

Voyage of the Little Mermaid

This show uses cartoons, live characters and Audio-Animatronics, as well as special effects with lasers and water to create an underwater grotto. Young children may find the lightning storm scary.

Attraction number		1	2	3	4	5	6	7	8	9	10
Minimum height:	(inches)	48	40	–	–	–	–	–	40	–	–
	(cm)	122	101						101		
Recommended age group		9+	9+	all	all	all	all	8+	8+	all	all
Duration (minutes)		3.5	4.5	30	40	25	35	15	10	30	17

Disney's Animal Kingdom® Park

As the name implies, wildlife rules at the latest addition to Disney's empire of fun. Here, the serious issue of conservation is combined with the playfulness of a theme park, though critics complain that the landscaping makes it hard to see the animals, especially in the hottest parts of the day. There's compensation in the fact that the park has some enthraling shows and rides, and rumor has it that future plans for a new zone include a roller coaster. For now, the park is all about getting back to nature, albeit of a more exotic kind than the one Florida usually has to offer.

Restaurantosaurus *(see p71)* serves up kid-friendly fast food for lunch and dinner.

The best times to see the animals are as soon as the park opens and within an hour of it closing, especially during the hot months (May–Sep).

Use FastPass *(see p132)*, a ride reservation system that helps cut the amount of time spent standing in line for the most popular rides and shows.

As in all Disney parks, smoking is allowed only in designated outdoor areas.

Savannah Circle, Walt Disney World Resort
• Map G1
• 407-824-4321
• www.disneyworld.com
• Open at least 8am–6pm, sometimes 7am–7pm. Call for seasonal hours.
• Adm: adults $79, children (3–9) $68 including tax. Children under 3 go free.

Top 10 Attractions

1. Kilimanjaro Safaris
2. Pangani Forest Exploration Trail
3. Festival of The Lion King
4. Kali River Rapids
5. Maharajah Jungle Trek
6. Tree of Life
7. It's Tough to Be a Bug!
8. Finding Nemo – The Musical
9. DINOSAUR
10. The Boneyard

1 Kilimanjaro Safaris

The park's most popular ride *(right)* puts you on a large safari jeep to bump along dirt tracks looking for black rhinos, lions, zebras, and more. You're reminded that it's a theme park, though, as a staged adventure unfolds – guests have to save the elephants from "poachers". The animals are real, but that baobab tree was made by Disney's Imagineers.

2 Pangani Forest Exploration Trail

As you're surrounded by thick vegetation, it's sometimes hard to see the animals on this walk-in-the-woods with a difference. The gorillas are the main attraction, but if the stars of the show prove shy, there are also hippos, exotic birds, and weird-looking mole-rats.

3 Festival of The Lion King

One of Orlando's best shows won't fail to throw you into the spirit of things when it gets going. This production uses singers, dancers, and The Lion King's popular score to emphasize nature's diversity.

4 Kali River Rapids

The park's conservation message is evident on this exciting raft ride, which passes from a lush landscape to one in the process of being scorched for logging. You need to be 38 inches (96 cm) tall or more to ride, and like to get wet!

For other Disney sights and attractions **See pp88–91**

Maharajah Jungle Trek
The giant Old World fruit bats, some with man-sized wingspans, are easily spotted, but the Bengal tigers are elusive when it's hot. You might also see Komodo dragons, tapirs, and deer in this atmospheric Asian stroll.

Tree of Life
The park's symbol is this 145-ft (44-m) tall tree created by Walt Disney Imagineers. Look carefully: there are 325 mammals, reptiles, amphibians, insects, birds, dinosaurs, and Mickeys carved into its trunk, limbs, and roots.

Disney's Animal Kingdom Park Plan

It's Tough to Be a Bug!
Located inside the Tree of Life's 50-ft (15-m) base, this 3-D, effect-filled show offers a view of the world from an insect's perspective. The climax is sure to make an impression.

Finding Nemo – The Musical
The Theater in the Wild is transformed into an enchanted undersea world for this original stage show, which merges puppetry with live performances. The show lasts for 30 minutes.

Park Guide
The park, which is Walt Disney World Resort's largest, is divided into six zones: Oasis (the entrance area); Discovery Island (with the Tree of Life at its center); and the lands of Camp Minnie-Mickey (the main children's zone), Africa, Asia, and Dinoland USA radiating out from it. Maps are available at Guest Relations, at the entrance to the park.

DINOSAUR
Expect to be shaken up on this wild ride, which takes you back 65 million years. Convincing animatronic dinosaurs lurk in the darkness. There's a 40-inch (102-cm) minimum height requirement.

The Boneyard
Possibly the best of its kind in any of the Disney parks, this playground is a perfect place for kids to burn off surplus energy. The play area is built around the "remains" of dinosaurs. It's both educational and fun.

Attraction number	1	2	3	4	5	6	7	8	9	10
Recommended age group	all	all	all	8+	all	all	all	all	9+	3 to 12
Duration (minutes)	14	–	28	5	–	–	7	30	4	–

For another conservation-oriented park **See pp28–31**

10 Islands of Adventure

Orlando didn't have a lot to offer adrenalin junkies until Universal unveiled its second Central Florida park in 1999. Billed as the "world's most technologically advanced theme park," no local rivals can touch Islands of Adventure's (IOA) thrill power and innovation (although Tampa's Busch Gardens [see p82] is also highly rated by thrill-seekers). With terrifying roller coasters, three heart-stopping water attractions, and stunningly creative rides, it is the place to head for those who like to live dangerously.

Green Eggs and Ham Café

⊙ Go on. Try a green eggs and ham sandwich at the Green Eggs and Ham Café.

⊙ The Universal Express system *(see p132)* cuts the amount of time spent standing in line for the most popular rides and shows.

Some of the park's rides have shorter lines for single guests and couples willing to split up.

During thunderstorms, the park's plentiful outdoor rides close.

⊛ Hollywood Way
• Map T1 • 407-363-8000 • www.universalorlando.com
• Open at least 9am–7pm, call for seasonal hours.
• Adm: adults $79, children (3–9) $69 (including tax), children under 3 go free.
• One-day tickets can be upgraded to a two-day pass if you find you want to spend another day in the park.

Top 10 Attractions
1. Incredible Hulk Coaster
2. The Amazing Adventures of Spider-Man
3. Doctor Doom's Fearfall
4. Pteranodon Flyers
5. Jurassic Park River Adventure
6. Popeye & Bluto's Bilge-Rat Barges
7. Dudley Do-Right's Ripsaw Falls
8. Dueling Dragons
9. Poseidon's Fury
10. The Cat in the Hat

The Amazing Adventures of Spider-Man
Slap on 3-D glasses and battle the baddies while fireballs and other computer-generated objects fly at you. The technology is amazing *(below)*.

Doctor Doom's Fearfall
This ride climbs 200 ft (61 m), before dropping and pausing at several levels to maximum thrilling effect.

Pteranodon Flyers
Eye-catching metal gondolas swing from side to side on this prehistoric bird's-eye tour around the park's Jurassic Park zone.

Incredible Hulk Coaster
You blast out of the darkness at 40 mph (64 kmph), go weightless, and endure seven inversions and two drops during this white-knuckle ride *(below)*.

Jurassic Park River Adventure
This ride starts slowly but quickly picks up speed as some raptors get loose *(below)*. To escape you will have to take an 85-ft (26-m), flume-style plunge.

Popeye & Bluto's Bilge-Rat Barges

The water is freezing on what is Florida's bounciest raft ride. Expect to be squirted, splashed, or even drenched as your 12-passenger "barge" goes the course.

Dudley Do-Right's Ripsaw Falls

Six-passenger logs cruise the lagoon before giving riders an excuse for a good squeal, a steep drop at 50 mph (80 kmph). The ride seems to finish up "underwater."

Islands of Adventure Park Plan

Park Guide

Despite the elevators and moving sidewalks, it can still take 20 minutes to get to the attractions from the parking lot. Try to arrive early; if you are staying in a Universal Resort, you can get in before other visitors and enjoy the benefits of free Universal Express access, which allows you to skip long lines by showing your room key. Other visitors can buy a Universal Express Plus Pass from as little as $20 plus tax.

Dueling Dragons

These two floorless coasters do five rollovers and come within 1 ft (30 cm) of each other no less than three times. If you are really coura-geous, go for seats in the front row.

Poseidon's Fury

Visitors tour the ruins of the ancient Temple of Poseidon before passing through a swirling vortex of water and looking on as all hell breaks loose when Poseidon and Zeus have an almighty battle.

The Cat in the Hat

Hold on as your couch spins and turns through 18 Seussian scenes. The Cat, Thing One, and Thing Two join you on a ride through a day that's anything but ordinary.

Attraction number		1	2	3	4	5	6	7	8	9	10
Minimum height:	(inches)	54	40	52	36	42	42	44	54	–	–
	(cm)	137	102	132	91	107	107	112	137		
Recommended age group		9+	8+	10+	7+	9+	9+	9+	9+	all	8+
Duration (minutes)		2	4	0.5	1.5	6.5	6.5	5.5	2.5	6	5

Left **One Fish, Two Fish....** Center **Dudley Do-Right** Right **Jurassic Park Discovery Center**

🔟 Gentler Attractions

1 One Fish, Two Fish, Red Fish, Blue Fish
Fly your fish up, down, and all around on an aerial carousel ride just 15 ft (4 m) off the ground. If you don't do what the song says, you'll get sprayed with water.

2 Caro-Seuss-El
This merry-go-round replaces the traditional horses with interactive versions of Dr. Seuss's cowfish, elephant birds, and mulligatawnies. Regular carousels will never seem the same again.

3 If I Ran the Zoo
The 19 interactive stations in this Seussian playground use features such as flying water snakes, caves, and water cannons, and include a place to tickle the toes of a Seussian critter.

4 Jurassic Park Discovery Center
See through a dinosaur's eyes, match your DNA to theirs, and watch an animatronic velociraptor "hatch" in the laboratory. There are several interactive stations, where kids can brush up on their dinosaur facts.

5 The Mystic Fountain
Make a wish at this fountain in Sinbad's Village. This wonderful fountain is interactive and is surprisngly playful, asking

questions of and teasing guests. Watch out that it doesn't spray you, so don't stand too close.

6 Camp Jurassic
Burn off energy in an adventure playground full of places to explore, including dark caves where "spitters" (small dinosaurs) lurk. See if you can find out how to make dinosaurs roar.

Triceratops Discovery Trail

7 Me Ship, The Olive
The play area here is full of interactive fun, while Cargo Crane offers an alternative hands-on experience: a chance to fire water cannons at riders on Popeye & Bluto's Bilge-Rat Barges *(see p21)*.

8 Flying Unicorn
Dueling Dragons *(see p21)* it ain't. This kiddie coaster has a gentle corkscrew action. Riders must be 36 inches (90 cm) tall.

9 The Eighth Voyage of Sinbad Stunt Show
This show is filled with stunts, giant flames, and explosions, as Sinbad hunts for lost treasure.

10 Storm Force Accelatron
Dizziness is the name of the game as you and X-Men superhero Storm spin your vehicle fast enough to create electrical energy that will send the evil Magneto to the great beyond.

Top 10 Facts

1. Steven Spielberg produced the 3-D films shown in Spider-Man.
2. Spider-Man's screens are up to 90 ft (27 m) wide.
3. The 15-Hz square audio wave shock used in Spider-Man is a frequency low enough to make humans sick.
4. Each "Scoop" on the Spider-Man ride actually only moves 12 inches (30 cm) up or down.
5. Dueling Dragons' Fire Dragon can travel at up to 60 mph (96 kmph), the Ice Dragon at up to 55 mph (88 kmph).
7. Dueling Dragons' structure is 3,200 ft (975 m) long and can handle 3,264 riders per hour.
8. At 3,180 ft (969 m), Dueling Dragons' line is the longest in the world.
9. The Hulk is 3,700 ft (1.1 km) long and can handle 1,920 riders per hour.
10. The Hulk's G-force is the same as that experienced in a F-16 fighter jet attack.

IOA's "State-of-the-Future" Rides

Guests at Islands of Adventure (IOA) get a first-hand demonstration of some of the most technologically advanced coasters and attractions ever created. At the top of the list is The Amazing Adventures of Spider-Man (see p20), a ride that took half a decade and more than $100 million to develop. New digital film technologies had to be invented for the convincing floor-to-ceiling 3-D images that are projected to a moving audience. The "Scoop" motion simulator, wind cannons, and pyrotechnics are precision-synchronized by a vast computer network. Computers also play a big part in the Dueling Dragons ride (see p21). They calculate the weight of every passenger load, then adjust the speed and departure sequence in order to maximize thrills on this duel coaster. Unique to the Incredible Hulk Coaster (see p20) is a thrust system that blasts cars out of a tunnel instead of the usual long, slow haul to the top of an incline. But even with all these high-tech innovations, some low-tech touches can't be avoided. Just below the Hulk stretches a huge net designed to catch personal belongings that fall from screaming riders.

The Incredible Hulk

Riders experience zero-gravity inversions as they are spun upside down at 110 ft (33 m) above the ground before dropping 105 ft (32 m) at more than 60 mph (96 kmph)

The Amazing Adventures of Spider-Man

Universal Studios Florida

Universal's first park in Florida opened in 1990, with movie-themed rides and shows, and a mission to steal some of Disney Hollywood's limelight. But it is only since a recent revamp that the park has really taken off, due largely to the runaway success of the hugely popular Men in Black Alien Attack, Terminator 2: 3-D, and the child-friendly Woody Woodpecker's KidZone.

The Universal globe

○ Don your movie star shades and grab a pastry and a cappuccino at the Beverly Hills Boulangerie.

○ The Universal Express ticket *(see p132)* lets you cut the amount of time spent in lines for the most popular rides and shows.

VIP tours *(see p129)* help beat the crowds during peak periods.

Note that some rides don't open until around 11am.

○ 1000 Universal Studios Plaza
• Map T1
• 407-363-8000
• www.universalorlando.com
• Open at least 9am–7pm but call to check seasonal hours.
• Adm: adults $79, children (3–9) $69 (including tax), children under 3 go free.

Top 10 Attractions

1 Terminator 2: 3-D
2 The Simpsons Ride
3 Men in Black Alien Attack
4 Twister – Ride It Out
5 Shrek 4-D
6 Jaws
7 Disaster!
8 Jimmy Neutron's Nicktoon Blast
9 Lucy: A Tribute
10 Revenge of The Mummy

Men in Black Alien Attack

You and your "alienator" must keep the intergalactic bad guys from taking over the world as you spin through the streets, looking to shoot the monstrous bugs *(below)*.

Twister – Ride It Out

The special effects make you feel as if a tornado is sucking the air out of the room as a 5-story funnel cloud really does make cows fly. Rated PG-13.

Terminator 2: 3-D

Live stage action, six 8-ft (2.4-m) robots, and an amazing three-screen, 3-D film *(below)* combine for a stunning, action-packed show (PG-13).

The Simpsons Ride

Swoop, soar, and smash your way through Krustyland on a motion simulator ride with Bart and the rest of the US's favorite cartoon family.

Shrek 4-D

This 13-minute fun-packed movie ride features excellent special effects, and is the bridge to Shrek 2, the next installment in the series.

For Universal's sister park, Islands of Adventure, See pp20–23

Universal Studios Florida Park Plan

Jaws
A leisurely boat tour turns into a nightmare when a large dorsal fin appears and Jaws attacks. This $45-million ride is even scarier after dark, but the special effects are spectacular at any time of the day.

Disaster!
This interactive ride gives visitors a walk-on role in some of the world's worst disasters, from fires and floods to earthquakes and subway accidents.

Park Guide
It takes about 20 minutes to get from the parking lot to the attractions. Once inside, if you feel disoriented, park hosts can advise you on how best to get from A to B. If you are staying at a Universal hotel, make use of the early admission perk; if you haven't got that option, try to arrive an hour before the park opens and hit the major rides first. The park tends to be quietest midweek, and the crowds seem to evaporate when it rains, so this park is a good bet in bad weather. While it's mostly a built up mix of soundstages, backlots, sets, and shops, there are some green areas in which to take time out.

Jimmy Neutron's Nicktoon Blast
Board your rocket and chase the evil Ooblar in this neutronic driving race through a universe filled with Nickelodeon characters, including SpongeBob, Hey Arnold, and Rugrats.

Lucy: A Tribute
Lucille Ball, star of the much loved I love Lucy show is remembered in this exhibition. Costumes, photographs, and awards are some of the items on display chronicling her remarkable life and career.

Revenge of The Mummy
This high-speed rollercoaster propels guests through Egyptian tombs to face their fears. "Dark ride" scenes and a revolutionary induction track ensures its popularity.

Attraction number		1	2	3	4	5	6	7	8	9	10
Minimum height:	(inches) (cm)	–	40 102	42 107	–	–	–	–	–	–	48 120
Recommended age group		all	8+	8+	8+	8+	8+	8+	8+	all	8+
Duration (minutes)		23	4	4	18	20	20	5	4	–	4

For more attractions in the International Drive area See pp96–9

Left **A Day in the Park with Barney** Right **Beetlejuice's Rock 'n Roll Graveyard Revue**

Shows & Kids' Stuff

1 Fear Factor Live
Do you have the nerve to participate in this extreme audience participation show? Perform all kinds of stunts as you compete against other guests. Unscripted and unpredictable.

2 Beetlejuice's Rock 'n Roll Graveyard Revue
Dracula, Wolfman, Frankenstein, and Beetlejuice rock the house with music and pyrotechnic special effects in an 18-minute show. Rated PG-13.

3 Curious George Goes To Town
Follow in the footsteps of that mischievous monkey Curious George at this interactive playground, which offers water-based fun and an arena with thousands of soft sponge balls.

4 Blues Brothers
Non-purist fans of this film, who don't need to see John Belushi and Dan Ackroyd in the key roles, will enjoy this foot-stomping 20-minute revue.

5 Animal Actors on Location
The park's newest show features wild, wacky, and occasionally weird live and video animal action. Expect plenty of audience participation.

6 Woody Woodpecker's Nuthouse Coaster
Very similar to the Barnstormer ride in Disney's Magic Kingdom (see p8), this 55-second ride for the young (and timid adults) has just one corkscrew curve.

7 E. T. Adventure
Everyone's favorite extra-terrestrial takes guests on a bike ride to save his planet. Peddle through strange landscapes to meet Tickli Moot Moot and other characters that Steven Spielberg created for this ride.

8 A Day in the Park with Barney
The puffy purple dinosaur is adored by preschool kids, so this 25-minute sing-along show is guaranteed to get small fans into a frenzy. Everyone else should probably steer clear.

9 Fievel's Playland
This partially hidden water playground has a house for kids to explore and a mini water slide, for which the line is often painfully slow.

Fievel's Playland

10 Kidzone Trolley Characters Meet and Greet
This is the place to come and meet some of your favorite cartoon characters. They will happily pose for photos and goof around with children.

For Orlando's best dinner shows See pp80–81

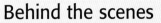

Top 10 TV Shows and Films made at Universal Studios Florida

1. Nickelodeon
2. Parenthood (1989)
3. Oscar (1990)
4. Psycho IV (1990)
5. Problem Child 2 (1991)
6. Matinee (1992)
7. The Waterboy (1998)
8. Hoover (1998)
9. House on Haunted Hill (1999)
10. Held for Ransom (2000)

Behind the scenes

Universal Studios Florida is more than just a tourist attraction. It is also the state's largest full-service studio facility and the heart of central Florida's burgeoning film and television production industry – an industry that rings Orlando's cash registers to the tune of nearly $500 million dollars annually. It's easy to see why the city is firmly in contention for the nickname "Hollywood East." Since opening in 1990, Universal Studios Florida has been the production site for thousands of television shows, commercials, music videos, and movies. As well as nine enormous soundstages, there are plenty of locations around the park that are used for filming, from downtown Manhattan to the Wild West. If park guests want to be part of some camera action, they can join the studio audience when TV shows shoot episodes at Universal. Tickets for these productions are typically distributed free of charge on the day of taping. Visitors can check in advance with Guest Services to find out if special event TV shows will be taped during their visit: shooting boards and the park map should also give up-to-date details.

Star Spotting

Universal Studios doesn't just allow you to "ride the movies". Here, you get to meet the stars, too. Actors playing a whole host of silver-screen and TV legends – including Marilyn Monroe, Scooby-Doo, SpongeBob SquarePants, and the Simpsons – can be seen around the park (especially in the Front Lot) and are always willing to pose for photos.

Hollywood Boulevard, Universal Studios Florida

⑩ SeaWorld Orlando

Opened in 1973, SeaWorld Orlando is the city's third major attraction. But its unique marine wildlife focus and educational goals puts it in a league all of its own. Guests can get up close and personal with killer whales, sea lions, manatees, rays, and a host of other watery creatures. The addition of thrill rides has expanded the park's appeal to teens, confirming SeaWorld as an essential part of any family's Orlando visit.

Journey to Atlantis ride

⭐ For lunch, head to Sharks Underwater Grill. This upscale restaurant offers fish and seafood and allows diners to eat under water, surrounded by creatures of the deep.

⭐ Get a Quick Queue ticket for special access *(see p132)*.

Beat the heat with mid-day visits to air-conditioned indoor attractions.

Didn't bring a stroller? Rent one at the Children's Store. Two-way radios can also be hired at the maps & education building.

🌐 7007 SeaWorld Dr
• Map T5
• 407-351-3600
• www.seaworldorlando.com/seaworld/fla
• Opens 9am, closes between 5pm and 10pm (depending on the season)
• Adm: adults $64.95, children (3–9) $53.95 (plus 6% tax). Children under 3 go free.

Top 10 Attractions
1 Dolphin Cove
2 Wild Arctic
3 Kraken
4 Journey to Atlantis
5 Believe
6 Shark Encounter
7 Manatee Rescue
8 Pacific Point Preserve
9 Manta
10 A'Lure

Wild Arctic
2 An impressive and chilly re-creation of the Arctic, with ice walls nearly a half-inch thick. See polar bears *(below)*, beluga whales, harbor seals, and walruses. Guests can opt to "arrive" by a simulated helicopter ride, but the line will be longer.

Kraken
3 Billed as the "tallest, fastest, longest, and only floorless roller coaster in Orlando," Kraken is a fearsome thrill. It takes riders up 15 stories, spins them upside down seven times, and goes under water, all at speeds up to 65 mph (104.6 kmph).

Dolphin Cove
1 The joyful spirit of "Flipper" lives on with these playful bottlenose dolphins *(below)*, which romp at the edge of the lagoon where they can be petted.

Journey to Atlantis
4 The big draw of this flume ride is a 60-ft (18-m) drop, but the surprise bonus is the twisting roller coaster section near the end. Everyone should expect to get wet, especially those in the front of the car.

Believe
5 This revolutionary show features SeaWorld's entire family of killer whales performing choreography to an original musical score with rotating panoramic screens.

Eingang

Zur Orientierung

Shark Encounter
In dem weltgrößten transparenten Unterwassertunnel kommen Besucher Haien bis auf 15 Zentimeter nahe *(oben)*. Per Förderband gleitet man durch die Welt der Aale, Kugelfische und Barrakudas.

Manatee Rescue
Die aufgrund von Verletzungen durch Schiffsschrauben vom Aussterben bedrohten Seekühe zählen zu den sanftesten Tieren der Erde. Manatee Rescue beherbergt gesundende Tiere.

Pacific Point Preserve
Die Hunderte Seelöwen und Robben auf den von Brandung umtosten Felsen, einer Kopie kalifornischer Küstenlandschaft, richten sich oft auf und fordern lautstark Futter.

Kurzführer

Die beim Information Counter erhältlichen Übersichtskarten mit Showzeiten sind hilfreich für die Planung des Besuchs. Vor den Fahrgeschäften Wild Arctic, Kraken und Journey to Atlantis bilden sich meist lange Warteschlangen. Während der Aufführungszeiten der großen Shows herrscht dort weniger Andrang. Spätnachmittags und abends befinden sich weniger Besucher im Park, die Temperaturen sind für die Besichtigung angenehm.

Manta
Die spannende Attraktion verbindet Lernen mit Spaß: Sie bietet wandhohe Aquarien und eine einzigartige Achterbahn *(links)*, in der Fahrgäste wie Mantarochen gleiten und tauchen.

A'Lure
Die aufregende Show im Nautilus Theater präsentiert faszinierende Luftartistik, Athletik, Akrobatik und Jo-Jo-Künstler. Sie erzählt die Geschichte der mythischen Sirenen, die Seemänner mit ihrem hypnotischen Gesang betörten, sodass diese Schiffbruch erlitten.

Seekühe sind die drittgrößten Meeressäuger der Welt. Entwicklungsgeschichtlich sind Elefanten ihre nächsten Verwandten.

Links **Dolphin Nursery** Rechts **Penguin Encounter**

Shows & andere Attraktionen

1 Pets Ahoy
18 Katzen, ein Dutzend Hunde, eine Vogelschar, Ratten, drei kleine Schweine und ein Pferd beweisen in einer lustigen Präsentation von Geschick und Tricks ihre Bühnentauglichkeit.

2 Shamu Close Up
Von dem Aussichtsbereich unter Wasser auf die Großen Schwertwale in SeaWorld erleben Besucher eine ganz besondere Darbietung: die Erziehungsversuche der Waleltern lassen sich hervorragend beobachten.

3 Penguin Encounter
In der Nachbildung des Polarmeeres und seiner verschneiten Ufer spielen, schwimmen und faulenzen mehr als 100 Pinguine aus der Arktis und drei weitere Vogelarten.

4 Blue Horizons
Delfine, Modelle von Großen Schwertwalen, erstklassige Taucher und Luftartisten in kunstvollen Kostümen harmonieren in einer atemberaubenden Show.

5 Stingray Lagoon
Vom Beckenrand aus kann man Stachelrochen aus ihren Verstecken locken. Die stets hungrigen Tiere sammeln sich bei Fisch reichenden Händen. Die Fütterungszeiten sind bei dem Fischverkaufsstand angeschlagen.

Stingray Lagoon

6 Dolphin Nursery
Wenn die Delfine des Parks Junge bekommen, werden sie in den schattigen Außenpool gebracht. Auf Anfrage erteilt das Personal gern Hintergrundinformationen.

7 Skytower
Den 137 Meter hohen Turm kann man auf Führungen erklimmen. Von der Spitze bietet sich eine wunderbare Aussicht auf den Park. Für die Besichtigung des Turms wird eine gesonderte Gebühr erhoben.

8 Clydesdale Hamlet
Das Clydesdale Hamlet bietet Abwechslung von den Meerestieren in SeaWorld. In den Ställen von Anheuser-Busch mit den berühmten Clydesdale-Pferden lassen sich viele Erinnerungsfotos schießen.

9 Shamu's Happy Harbor
Wenn Kinder die Konzentration verlässt, bietet der riesige Spielplatz mit Rutschen, einem kleinen Wasserpark, einem Labyrinth aus Netzen, Steel Drums und einem eigenen Sandkasten für die Kleinsten Ablenkung.

10 Caribbean Tidepool
In der natürlichen Lagune mit Strand, Dünen und endemischen Pflanzen leben bedrohte Arten von Wasserschildkröten.

Schwimmen mit Delfinen in Discovery Cove **siehe S. 97**

Top 10 gefährdete Tierarten in SeaWorld Orlando

1 Meeresschildkröten *(Cheloniidae)*
2 Seekühe *(Trichechus)*
3 Zwergpottwale *(Kogia breviceps)*
4 Kleinstpottwale *(Kogia simus)*
5 Grindwale *(Globicephala)*
6 Große Tümmler *(Tursiops truncatus)*
7 Große Schwertwale *(Orcinus orca)*
8 Kanadakraniche *(Grus canadensis)*
9 Reiher *(Ardeidae)*
10 Grackeln *(Quiscalus)*

Tierschutz in SeaWorld Orlando

Das Personal von SeaWorld Orlando lehrt nicht nur Große Schwertwale, das Publikum auf Kommando nass zu spritzen. Im Rahmen ihres Schutzauftrages befinden sich die Tierexperten der SeaWorld Parks in Orlando, Texas und Kalifornien in 24-stündiger Rufbereitschaft, um kranke oder verletzte Meeressäuger, Vögel und Schildkröten zu retten. Die Tiere werden in den Parks gepflegt und nach Möglichkeit wieder in ihren natürlichen Lebensraum eingegliedert. Die gefährdeten Seekühe sind regelmäßig Gäste in SeaWorld: Jedes Jahr werden zahlreiche Tiere durch Schiffsschrauben, Angelschnüre und Toxide verletzt oder getötet. Nach Eingang eines Notrufs leistet ein SeaWorld-Team mit spezieller Ausrüstung Erste Hilfe vor Ort. Gesundende Seekühe sind in der Abteilung Manatee Rescue zu sehen (siehe S.29). Seit Einführung des Schutzprogramms 1976 wurden durch SeaWorld Orlando mehr als 270 Seekühe gerettet, mehr als 100 wurden wieder in ihren natürlichen Lebensraum eingegliedert. Ende des Jahres 2000 betrug die Anzahl der durch SeaWorld Orlando geretteten Tiere verschiedener Arten 3251, 735 wurden wieder ausgesetzt.

Aufzuchtprogramm

SeaWorld betreibt ein äußerst erfolgreiches Aufzuchtprogramm: Pinguine, Robben und mehr als zehn Große Schwertwale wurden in SeaWorld Orlando geboren.

SeaWorld-Mitarbeiter entlassen drei Seekühe in die Freiheit

Folgende Doppelseite **Kraken, SeaWorld Orlando**

31

🔟 Wet 'n Wild®

Der 1977 von George Millay, dem Gründer von SeaWorld Orlando, eröffnete Vergnügungspark bietet zahlreiche Fahrgeschäfte und Familienattraktionen. Besucher schätzen die mit einer Strandparty vergleichbare Atmosphäre. Obwohl der Park inzwischen von Universal Studios Florida® übernommen wurde, ist der kommerzielle Charakter wenig ausgeprägt. Der Schwerpunkt liegt auf den rasanten, atemberaubenden Fahrten. Trotz Konkurrenz durch Disney's Blizzard Beach und Typhoon Lagoon bleibt Wet 'n Wild® der aufregendste Wasserpark der Region.

Surf Lagoon

🅑 **Bubba's Bar-B-Q & Chicken** serviert gutes Mittagessen. Die Imbissstände im Park akzeptieren gängige Kreditkarten.

⊘ Treppen und Wege können sehr heiß werden. Rutschsichere Badeschuhe sind empfehlenswert.

Um bei schnellen Fahrten keine Blöße zu zeigen, sollten Frauen Badeanzüge statt Bikinis tragen.

Kinder müssen mindestens 91 Zentimeter groß sein, um allein fahren zu dürfen.

- 6200 International Dr
- Karte T2
- 407 351 1800
- www.wetnwildorlando.com
- tägl. 10–17 Uhr; aktuelle Öffnungszeiten tel. erfragen
- Eintritt: Erwachsene 47,87 $, Kinder (3–9 Jahre) 41,48 $ (inkl. Steuern), Kinder unter 3 Jahren frei
- Halbtageskarten (nachmittags) sind ganzjährig verfügbar

Top 10 Wasserspaß

1. Der Stuka/The Bomb Bay
2. The Storm
3. The Black Hole™
4. Disco H2O™
5. Mach 5
6. The Flyer
7. Lazy River
8. Bubba Tub®
9. Bubble Up
10. Brain Wash™

1 Der Stuka / The Bomb Bay

Mutige können zwischen der 15 Meter hohen Rutsche Der Stuka mit einem Gefälle von 78 Grad und der gleich hohen, aber noch steileren Bomb Bay *(unten)* wählen.

2 The Storm

Die Schussfahrt führt durch Nebel, Donner und Blitze. Passagiere wirbeln durch ein offenes Becken, bevor sie in den tiefer liegenden Pool fallen.

3 The Black Hole®

Auf Reifen für zwei Personen geht es in vollkommener Dunkelheit 153 Meter durch gewundene Röhren *(rechts)*.

4 Disco H2O

Jeweils vier Passagiere steuern auf einem Reifen durch die Röhre mit Disco-Atmosphäre. Dabei spielt Musik aus den 1970er Jahren.

⟹ *Mehr über Wet 'n Wild®*
www.universalorlando.com/amusement-parks/wet-n-wild.html

Mach 5
5 Es macht Spaß, in den Steilkurven der Fahrt mit den Schaumstoffunterlagen möglichst hoch zu gleiten.

Eingang

Zur Orientierung

The Flyer
6 Auf einem Reifen sausen vier Personen zusammen wie auf einer Rodelbahn 137 Meter lang durch Kurven und über gerade Strecken.

Lazy River
7 Die rundumlaufende, 1,6 Kilometer lange Wasserstecke *(links)* windet sich an Palmen, tropischen Pflanzen und Wasserfällen vorbei. Auf der Bahn kann man wunderbar schwimmen oder langsam und entspannt auf einem Reifen zum Ausgangspunkt zurückgleiten.

Bubba Tub®
8 Die 15 Meter hohe Rutsche *(links)* beinhaltet drei Steilstücke. Auf den vier Personen fassenden Reifen können Familien die Fahrt zusammen genießen.

Kurzführer
Die gewaltige Surf Lagoon bildet den Mittelpunkt von Wet 'n Wild®. Die Fahrgeschäfte sind kreisförmig um die Surf Lagoon angeordnet. In den Schließfächern beim »Tube, Towel & Locker Rental« rechts des Parkeingangs können Besucher persönliche Gegenstände aufbewahren. Die Guest Services befinden sich links des Eingangs. Es empfiehlt sich, rechtzeitig einen Liegestuhl mit einem Handtuch zu belegen, um zwischen den Fahrten einen Platz zum Sonnen und Entspannen zur Verfügung zu haben.

Bubble Up
9 Bei dem Spiel für Kinder bis zwölf Jahren klettern die Teilnehmer an einem Seil auf einen großen Ballon. Wer dabei abrutscht, landet in einem 91 Zentimeter tiefen Becken. Wasserpistolen tragen zu dem großen Durcheinander bei und sorgen für eine Extraportion Spaß.

Brain Wash™
10 Am Ende der extrem schnellen Fahrt *(oben)* stürzen die Passagiere auf zwei bis vier Personen fassenden Reifen 16 Meter tief in ein überkuppeltes Becken. Fahrgäste müssen mindestens 1,20 Meter groß sein.

Weitere Erlebnisbäber in Orlando **siehe S. 48f**

10 Merritt Island

Dank des Engagements der US-Regierung in der Raumfahrt entstand mit dem Merritt Island National Wildlife Refuge beim Kennedy Space Center das zweitgrößte Naturschutzgebiet Floridas. Das 1963 als Sicherheitszone für die NASA angelegte, über 560 Quadratkilometer große Areal ist heute wichtiger Lebensraum für gefährdete Arten und Hunderte Zugvögel. Die Seekühe sind die größte Attraktion des Parks.

Beginn des Wildlife Drive

🅠 Nehmen Sie, bevor Sie auf die Insel übersetzen, einen Imbiss von Paul's Smoke House an der Indian River Lagoon mit.

🅒 Auf dem Black Point Wildlife Drive lassen sich Wildtiere am besten ein bis zwei Stunden nach Sonnenaufgang und ein bis zwei Stunden vor Sonnenuntergang beobachten, wenn sie auf dem Weg zu den Futterplätzen sind.

• östl. von Titusville auf der SR 402; Ausfahrt 220 von der 1-95, dann 6,5 km (4 Meilen) auf der SR 402 (Garden Street) in östlicher Richtung
• 312 861 0667
• www.fws.gov/merritt island/ oder www.nbbd.com/godo/minwr
• ganzjährig geöffnet
• geschl. an US-Feiertagen & vier Tage vor Raketenstarts
• Eintritt frei

Top 10 Natur

1. Seekühe
2. Black Point Wildlife Drive
3. Angeln
4. Bootstour
5. Vogelbeobachtung
6. Wandern
7. Jagen
8. Besucherzentrum
9. Zugvögel & Schildkröten
10. Strände

1 Seekühe

Seekühe sind ganzjährig, im Frühjahr und Herbst aber besonders zahlreich im Park vertreten. Man kann die pflanzenfressenden Tiere am Banana River oder von der Plattform am Haulover Canal beobachten.

2 Black Point Wildlife Drive

Der elf Kilometer (sieben Meilen) lange, leicht begehbare Rundweg verbindet Aussichtsplätze, von denen aus sich wunderbar Wasser-, Wat- und Raubvögel beobachten lassen.

3 Angeln

Um in Indian River, Banana River und Mosquito Lagoon nach Snooks, Roten Trommlern und gefleckten Umberfischen zu angeln, ist eine Genehmigung des Staates Florida und der Parkverwaltung erforderlich.

4 Bootstour

Auf Boots- oder Kanufahrten kommt man den Tieren ganz nahe: Je nach Saison sind zahllose Zugvögel an den Wasserstraßen zu sehen, Seekühe schwimmen unter Wasser.

Seekühe in Tampa's Lowry Park Zoo siehe S. 82

5 Vogelbeobachtung

Auf geführten Touren erläutern ehrenamtliche Mitarbeiter ungeübten Besuchern, woran einzelne Vogelarten zu erkennen sind, etwa am Beispiel des Schmuckreihers *(unten)*.

Zur Orientierung

6 Wandern

Es gibt sechs Wanderwege von einem halben bis acht Kilometer Länge. Die Wanderungen sind wenig anstrengend, allerdings wird man dabei etwas nass.

7 Jagen

Von November bis Januar ist auf Merritt Island die Jagd auf Enten und Blässhühner gestattet. Dazu sind Jagderlaubnis und Jagdschein erforderlich. Alle Jagdausflüge im Park müssen am frühen Nachmittag beendet sein.

8 Besucherzentrum

Neben einem 20-minütigen Film bieten Ausstellungen über Wildtiere und Schautafeln eine gute Einführung in das Merrit Island Wildlife Refuge. In den Teichen hinter dem Besucherzentrum sind häufig Alligatoren zu sehen.

Audioführer

Das Besucherzentrum bietet für die Fahrten auf dem Black Point Wildlife Drive Audioführer an. Am Eingang des Weges sind Broschüren für die Tourplanung erhältlich, in denen die besten Plätze für die Tierbeobachtung angegeben sind. Wenn Sie die Broschüre nicht behalten wollen, hinterlassen Sie sie in der Box am Ausgang für nachfolgende Besucher.

9 Zugvögel & Schildkröten

Das ganze Jahr über machen Tiere auf ihren Wanderungen im Park Station: Im Mai sind viele Vögel, im September Wasservögel zu sehen. Im Juni und Juli kommen Schildkröten zur Eiablage an die Strände.

10 Strände

Besucher des Parks verbringen gern mehr Zeit an Land als im Wasser. Badewillige finden am Playalinda Beach alle Einrichtungen vor. Achten Sie entlang der Straße zum Strand jedoch auf Alligatoren *(links)*.

Weitere Parks & Naturschutzgebiete siehe S.52f

🔟 Kennedy Space Center

Stärker als alle anderen Attraktionen in Florida betont das Kennedy Space Center die Errungenschaften menschlicher Neugier und Vorstellungskraft. Das 1967 errichtete Besucherzentrum der Anlage zählt zu den beliebtesten Sehenswürdigkeiten Floridas: Jedes Jahr gewinnen mehr als 1,5 Millionen Gäste Einblick in das Leben außerhalb der Erde. Außerdem ist das Gelände Schauplatz der beeindruckenden Starts von SpaceShuttles.

Vehicle Assembly Building

🔴 **Genießen Sie im Moon Rock Café einen HotDog neben echtem Mondgestein.**

🔵 **Kennedy Space Center Tours bietet Tickets und einen Transportservice zum Besucherzentrum von verschiedenen Stellen in Orlando und Kissimmee (Informationen unter 888 838 8915 oder www. kennedyspacecenter tours.net)**

• Rte 405, Titusville
• außerhalb der Karte
• 321 449 4444 • www. kennedyspacecenter. com • tägl. 9–18.30 Uhr
• Eintritt: Erwachsene 38 $; Kinder (3–11 Jahre) 28 $, Kinder unter 2 Jahren frei • Tickets für Raketenstarts müssen im Voraus erworben werden; Informationen unter 321 449 4400 und www. kennedyspacecenter. com • Erkundigen Sie sich telefonisch nach Führungen

Top 10 Raumfahrt

1. Raketenstarts
2. Cape Canaveral: Then & Now Tour
3. Shuttle Launch Experience
4. Astronaut Encounter
5. LC-39 Observation Gantry
6. IMAX-Kinos
7. International Space Station Center
8. Apollo/Saturn V Center
9. Rocket Garden
10. Early Space Exploration

1 Raketenstarts
Einem Raketenstart beizuwohnen *(unten)* ist ein einzigartiges und unvergessliches Erlebnis. Die Website des Centers liefert aktuelle Termine der Shuttle-Starts.

2 Cape Canaveral: Then & Now Tour
Die dreistündige Tour führt zu historischen Abschussrampen und zum US Air Force Space & Missile Museum.

3 Shuttle Launch Experience
In der Simulation *(oben)* erleben Besucher die einzigartige Atmosphäre eines Raketenstarts mit allen visuellen und akustischen Eindrücken.

4 Astronaut Encounter
Das Kennedy Space Center ist der einzige Ort der Welt, an dem Besucher täglich echten Astronauten begegnen *(rechts)*. Erwachsene und Kinder finden die 30-minütige Fragerunde spannend.

5 LC-39 Observation Gantry
Der Turm bietet Blick auf die Raketenbauhalle und den »Crawlerway«, eine achtspurige Autobahn, auf der Raketen mit 1,6 km/h zur Abschussrampe transportiert werden.

IMAX-Kinos

Die beiden IMAX-Kinos im Kennedy Space Center zeigen zwei Filme: *Space Station – 3-D* und *Magnificent Desolation: Walking on the Moon 3-D*. In Letzterem begleiten Besucher Astronauten auf einer realen Reise auf den Mond.

Zur Orientierung

International Space Station Center

Besucher können der Vorbereitung von Komponenten für Raketenstarts beiwohnen. Einige Abteilungen der ISS sind in Originalgröße nachgebildet.

Apollo / Saturn V Center

Im Firing Room Theater erleben Besucher den historischen Start der Apollo 8 und können eine der drei noch existierenden Saturn-V-Raketen betrachten *(oben)*.

Rocket Garden

Der außergewöhnliche »Garten« *(rechts)* beherbergt acht Raketen, einschließlich einer Mercury Atlas. Dieser Raketentyp kam bei der Mission des Astronauten John Glenn zum Einsatz. Die Rot-weiß-blaue Beleuchtung verleiht der Präsentation patriotisches Flair.

Early Space Exploration

Besucher sehen die originalen Kontrollpanele der Mercury-Mission und weitere Gegenstände, die bei den ersten bemannten Raumfahrten der USA verwendet wurden. Die Raumfahrtprogramme Mercury und Gemini werden erläutert.

Kurzführer

Das Kennedy Space Center nimmt einen Teil des 45 Autominuten von Orlando entfernten Merritt Island National Wildlife Refuge *(siehe S. 36f)* ein. Die Busfahrt zu Ausstellungen außerhalb des Besucherzentrums ist im Eintrittspreis inbegriffen. Busse starten im Besucherzentrum am Information Center. Abgesehen von Tagen, an denen Raketenstarts stattfinden, ist der Besucherandrang im Kennedy Space Center überschaubar.

Geschichte der amerikanischen Raumfahrtprogramme
http://spaceflight.nasa.gov/history

39

Links **Saturn V** Mitte **X-15** Rechts **Von einer Titan-II-Trägerrakete abgesprengte Gemini-VII-Kapsel**

Raketen

Jupiter C
Der Vorläufer der Mercury Redstone *(siehe unten)* wurde unter der Leitung des deutschen Wissenschaftlers Wernher von Braun entwickelt. Die Jupiter C transportierte am 31. Januar 1958 den ersten amerikanischen Satelliten ins All.

X-15
Das Raketenflugzeug X-15 flog von 1959 bis 1968 199 Missionen. An Bord waren berühmte Astronauten wie Neil Armstrong. Die X-15 erreichte Höhen von 10,8 Kilometer und Geschwindigkeiten von bis zu 7274 km/h.

Mercury Redstone
Die Rakete brachte 1961 den ersten amerikanischen Astronauten in den Weltraum. Der Flug von Alan Shepard in einer Freedom-7-Kapsel dauerte 15 Minuten und 22 Sekunden.

Mercury Atlas
Als das Mercury-Programm nach sechs Flügen höhere Umlaufbahnen ansteuerte, wurde die Mercury Redstone durch die schubstärkere Mercury Atlas ersetzt. 1962 und 1963 gelangten die Astronauten John Glenn, Scott Carpenter, Wally Schirra und Gordon Cooper mit dieser Rakete ins All.

Titan II
Die Titan bot erstmals Platz für zwei Astronauten. Mit dem Raketentyp wurden 1965 und 1966 zehn bemannte Flüge durchgeführt.

Saturn 1B
In Vorbereitung der Mondlandung trug die Saturn 1B Apollo-Raumschiffe in die Erdumlaufbahn. Später wurden durch drei Missionen mit der Rakete die Raumfahrtstation Skylab bemannt (1973) und Astronauten zum Apollo-Sojus-Test-Projekt gebracht (1975).

Saturn V
Die mit 110 Metern Länge bisher größte Trägerrakete trug 1969 Apollo 11 ins All. Bei dieser Mission landeten Buzz Aldrin und Neil Armstrong auf dem Mond.

Titan Centaur
Mit der Rakete wurden 1977 die Raumsonden Voyager I und II auf eine Mission zu den Planeten Jupiter, Saturn, Uranus und Neptun gebracht.

Mercury Redstone

Pegasus
Mit der meist von Flugzeugen des Typs L-1011 aus startenden Trägerrakete gelangen Kommunikationssatelliten in die Erdumlaufbahn.

X-43A Launch Vehicle
Die Raketen könnten in Zukunft unbemannte Flugzeuge in extreme Höhen bringen, um so die Sicherheit der bemannten Raumfahrt zu verbessern.

Bilder von den Apollo-Missionen http://apollo.sese.asu.edu

Top 10 Bemannte Raumfahrt in den USA

SpaceShuttles

Die drei Space Shuttles Atlantis, Discovery *und* Endeavor *gehören aufgrund ihrer aktuellen und zukünftigen Bedeutung für die Raumfahrt zu den bekanntesten Fluggeräten der NASA. Die* Endeavour *ersetzte die Raumfähre* Challenger, *die auf ihrer 51. Mission am 28. Januar 1986 nur 73 Sekunden nach dem Start explodierte. Dabei starben alle sieben Besatzungsmitglieder. 1988 wurden die Shuttle-Flüge nach eingehenden Sicherheitsprüfungen wieder aufgenommen. Im Weltraum erreichen die Raumfähren Geschwindigkeiten von bis zu 28 163 km/h. Im Frachtraum von der Größe eines Reisebusses (18,3 mal 4,6 Meter) können bis zu 22,5 Tonnen Material transportiert werden. Trotz ihrer Größe gleiten die antriebslosen Raumfähren elegant zurück zur Erde – ein Pelikan landet weniger sanft auf dem Wasser.*

Der 100. Start eines SpaceShuttles

Experimente im Weltraum
In den SpaceShuttles führen Astronauten eine Vielzahl von Versuchen durch. Am 20. April 1998 bereitete Kathryn Hire an Bord des Shuttles *Columbia* ein Schlafexperiment im sogenannten Neurolab vor *(rechts).*

Links **Dueling Dragons** Rechts **The Incredible Hulk Roller Coaster, beide Islands of Adventure**®

🔟 Achterbahnen

1 Splash Mountain®
Bei der Fahrt wird man zwangsläufig nass. Im Sommer ist die Abkühlung willkommen. Der Achterbahn von der Brücke zwischen Frontierland und Adventureland aus zuzusehen, ist zu jeder Jahreszeit attraktiv. Auch dabei bekommt man Wasser ab *(siehe S. 8, Magic Kingdom® Park)*.

2 The Twilight Zone Tower of Terror™
Besucher stürzen den Aufzugsschacht hinab, der in die Twilight Zone des Hollywood Hotels führt. Der Sage nach verschwanden in dem realen Hotel bei einem Gewitter 1939 fünf Aufzugpassagiere. Die Fahrt ist für kleine Kinder ungeeignet *(siehe S. 16, Disney Hollywood Studios™)*.

3 Rock 'n' Roller Coaster®
Die Beschleunigung der mit je 24 Fahrgästen besetzten »Limousinen« entspricht der eines Kampfflugzeugs. In jedem Wagen dröhnen aus 120 Lautsprechern Aerosmith-Hits *(siehe S. 16, Disney's Hollywood Studios™)*.

4 The Incredible Hulk Coaster®
In der rasanten Achterbahn erleben Passagiere eine schwerelose Fahrt durch mehrfache Loopings. Ein Fangnetz sammelt verloren gegangene Habe auf *(siehe S. 20, Islands of Adventure®)*.

5 Dueling Dragons®
Die beiden Züge beginnen die wilde Fahrt auf einer Höhe von über 30 Metern. Auf den äußeren Plätzen der ersten acht Reihen ist der Nervenkitzel bei den Beinahezusammenstößen am größten. Die Zentrifugalkräfte bei der Fahrt sind enorm *(siehe S. 21, Islands of Adventure®)*.

Dr Doom's Fearfall

6 The Amazing Adventures of Spider-Man®
Die technisch innovative Attraktion ist weniger turbulent als die Achterbahnen Dueling Dragons und The Incredible Hulk Coaster, für Besucher mit Herz- oder Gleichgewichtsstörungen dennoch nicht zu empfehlen *(siehe S. 20, Islands of Adventure®)*.

7 Doctor Doom's Fearfall®
Bei dem freien Fall in einem Metallkäfig baumeln die Beine in der Luft. Die vielen abrupten

Kraken, SeaWorld Orlando

 Mehr über Wasserparks in & um Orlando
www.watermania-florida.com

Stops auf der Fahrt entlocken den Passagieren manchen Schrei *(siehe S. 20, Islands of Adventure®)*.

Dudley Do-Right's Ripsaw Falls®

Das Fahrgeschäft wirkt auf den ersten Blick harmlos. Der Absturz, bei dem Rauch und durch Spiegel erzeugte Spezialeffekte die Illusion erzeugen, man würde einige Meter unter der Wasseroberfläche landen, macht Besucher jedoch atemlos *(siehe S. 20, Islands of Adventure®)*.

Kraken

Die Wagen mit je 32 Fahrgästen stürzen aus einer Höhe von 46 Metern mit einer Höchstgeschwindigkeit von 104 km/h 44 Meter in die Tiefe. Anschließend sausen die Fahrgäste auf der 1273 Meter langen Strecke durch sieben Loopings. Mancher Besucher erlebt die Achterbahnfahrt als die längsten 3 Minuten und 39 Sekunden seines Lebens *(siehe S. 28, SeaWorld Orlando)*.

Summit Plummet

Das Ende der 36 Meter langen wilden Wasserfahrt bildet eine mit 96 km/h durchfahrene Fallstrecke. Die Passagiere mit einer Mindestgröße von 122 Zentimetern brauchen Nervenstärke *(siehe S. 89, Blizzard Beach)*.

Top 10 Achterbahnen für Kinder

The Barnstormer at Goofy's Wiseacre Farm

Die einmütige Achterbahnfahrt bereitet großes Vergnügen *(siehe S. 8)*.

Cinderella's Golden Carrousel

Das 100 Jahre alte Karussell hat ein bezauberndes Märchenthema *(siehe S. 9)*.

The Many Adventures of Winnie the Pooh

1999 ersetzte das Fahrgeschäft den beliebten Mr. Toad's Wild Ride. Inzwischen hat Winnie the Pooh viele Fans *(siehe S. 9)*.

The Magic Carpets of Aladdin

Das Fahrgeschäft ist der erste Neuzugang in Adventureland seit 30 Jahren *(siehe S. 9)*.

Flying Unicorn

Die Achterbahn ist bei Kindern ebenso beliebt wie The Barnstormer und Woody's Nuthouse *(siehe S. 22)*.

Pteranodon Flyers®

Bei dem luftigen Abenteuer wird manchem Fahrgast flau im Magen *(siehe S. 20)*.

The Cat in the Hat™

Die Fahrt durch den sieben Meter langen Tunnel sorgt für Schwindelgefühl *(siehe S. 21)*.

Caro-Seuss-El

Das einzigartige Karussell besitzt Figuren aus Seuss-Geschichten *(siehe S. 22)*.

E. T. Adventure®

Die Fahrradtour durch fantastische Szenen lockt zahlreiche Besucher an *(siehe S. 26)*.

Woody Woodpecker's Nuthouse Coaster

Die Steilwandkurven der Miniaturachterbahn sorgen für großes Fahrvergnügen *(siehe S. 26)*.

Informationen über Fahrten in Achterbahnen für Kinder siehe S. 139

Links **Titanic – The Experience** Rechts **Ripley's Believe It Or Not! Odditorium**

10 Kleine Attraktionen

1 Gatorland®
In dem Park lauern rund 800 Alligatoren. Manche Tiere vollführen Tricks. Sie springen zum Beispiel nach Hühnchen, die Mitarbeiter als Futter über das Becken halten. Gatorland beherbergt außerdem ca. 200 Krokodile, einige Schlangen und andere Reptilien. Zur Anlage gehört auch der Wasserpark Gator Gully Splash mit vergnüglichen Fahrgeschäften *(siehe S. 107)*.

2 The Holy Land Experience
Rekonstruktionen des Grabs Jesu, des Herodianischen Tempels und der Höhlen, in denen die Schriftrollen vom Toten Meer entdeckt wurden, lassen das antike Jerusalem wiederauferstehen. Schauspieler stellen Bibelszenen nach und erzählen Geschichten aus dem Alten und dem Neuen Testament. The Holy Land Experience ist sowohl für Christen als auch für Angehörige anderer Religionen interessant. Ein Café serviert u. a. »Goliath Burger« *(siehe S. 98)*.

3 Ripley's Believe It or Not! Odditorium®
Von außen wirkt das Gebäude, als würde es im Boden versinken. Im Inneren sorgen Repliken menschlicher und tierischer Kuriositäten wie die einer doppelköpfigen Katze für Gänsehaut. In einem Film sind Kleiderhaken und Glühbirnen schluckende Menschen zu sehen. Auch eine *Mona Lisa* aus Toastscheiben gehört zu den verrückten Exponaten *(siehe S. 98)*.

4 Titanic – The Experience
Auf der Nachbildung der Titanic ist fast die Anwesenheit von Leonardo DiCaprio spürbar. Auf den geführten Touren stellen Schauspieler Passagiere und Besatzung dar. Die unter den 200 Exponaten befindlichen originalen Schwimmwesten vermitteln ein beklemmendes Gefühl *(siehe S. 99)*.

5 Fun Spot Action Park
Wer sich ein Leben auf der Überholspur wünscht, kann im Fun Spot Action Park dem Geschwindigkeitsrausch frönen: Auf den vier großen Kartbahnen geben die Fahrer Gas und jagen durch waghalsige Kurven zum Ziel. Die Anlage beherbergt auch Autoskooter, Boote, ein Riesenrad und eine Spielhalle mit Simulatoren *(siehe S. 97)*.

Gatorland

Titanic – The Experience
www.titanictheexperience.com

SkyVenture

If you've always wanted to try sky-diving but don't like the thought of stepping out of a plane, this vertical wind tunnel is for you. More than 100,000 visitors each year immerse themselves in the high adventure of skydiving without ever having to pack a parachute. There are certain weight restrictions and you have to be more than three years old, but other than that no experience is necessary. The price includes a class, gear and equipment, and two one-minute jumps, which is usually more than enough to exhaust a novice skydiver. ◈ 6805 Visitors Circle • 800-759-3861 • Map T2 • Open 10am–10pm daily • Adm • www.skyventure.com

SkyVenture

A World of Orchids

Orchids come in a multitude of strange shapes and colors, all of which are on display at this working greenhouse, home to 1,000 of the exotic flowers. Lush paths, serene streams, and the occasional squawk from a parrot offer respite from the busy hub-bub of the theme parks. See p107.

WonderWorks

Gimmicks abound inside this building, which, like Ripley's, is sinking into the ground, only this time it's roof first. Inside, there's an interactive arcade of some mild scientific educational value. Among the more than 85 hands-on activities, the curious can experience an earthquake or virtual hang gliding, and test their reflexes. For simple fun, the huge laser-tag field is a blast. See p99.

Reptile World Serpentarium

This unique and educational attraction gives visitors the opportunity to watch a snake handler in action as he extracts poisonous venom from deadly snakes. It also contains the largest reptile exhibit in Florida. See p108.

Winter Park Scenic Boat Tour

Glide through three of Winter Park's lakes on a pontoon boat for this hour-long tour. Nature-lovers can spot birds such as ospreys and herons. The more materialis-tic can swoon over huge lake-side mansions, sometimes getting close enough to peek in a window. The architecture of Rollins College, and the secluded feel of the canals, make this tour a popular option for the kitsch-weary. See p119.

Left **Swan Boats, Lake Eola** Right **Citywalk**

🔟 Ways to Have Fun on the Cheap

1 The Peabody Ducks
It all began in the 1930s when a couple of inebriated sportsmen returning from a week-end hunting trip thought it would be funny to put live ducks in the Peabody Hotel's lobby fountain. The joke stuck and now the original ducks' descendants are local celebrities. They march down from their penthouse at 11am, via the elevator, and return at 5pm. ◐ *9801 International Dr • Map T4 • 407-352-4000 • Free • www.peabodyorlando.com*

2 HOB Blues Bar
The main room at House of Blues is one of the best spots in town to catch big-name acts *(see p74)*. But the HOB Blues Bar, next door, is an intimate stage for small-scale blues bands that are generally unknown but excellent. Guests ordering dinner get priority for table seating. ◐ *Downtown Disney Westside • Map G2 • 407-934-2583 • Open 11am–11.30pm Sun–Wed (to 1:30am Thu–Sat) • Free*

The Peabody Ducks

3 Silver Spurs Rodeo
Located inside of Osceola Heritage Park, the Silver Spurs Arena seats 8,300 people. The Silver Spurs Rodeo was founded in 1944 by the Silver Spurs Riding Club to promote good horse-riding skills. The rodeo has bareback bronc riding, barrel racing, bull riding, saddle bronc, steer wrestling, team roping, and tie-down roping. It is the oldest rodeo in the Kissimmee-St. Cloud area. *See p109.*

4 Downtown Disney
With three parts – Westside, Marketplace, and Pleasure Island – glittering Downtown Disney has become the epicenter of nightlife at "the Mouse". Pleasure Island is currently undergoing major renovations, with the addition of new restaurants and shops. Both Westside and Marketplace are packed day and night. Hordes of guests (especially families) stroll among the area's shops and restaurants – it's bustling, fun, and costs little to enjoy. Kids in particular like the LEGO Store's *(see p92)* outdoor work stations.

5 Disney's BoardWalk
Almost an accidental attraction, this is a re-creation of a 1940s seaside resort, complete with street performers, carnival games, great restaurants and bars. The ESPN Club is the perfect spot to draw on a beer and catch a major-league game on big-screen TVs. *See p93.*

Center for Birds of Prey

Founded by the Florida Audubon Society, and off the beaten tourist track, this center's primary function is to rescue and rehabilitate wounded and orphaned raptors. Birds of prey that can't be released back into the wild, however, are kept and used to educate the public about wildlife conservation. With knowledgeable staff and the opportunity to stand close to birds such as eagles and vultures, the center is a captivating treat for a handful of dollars. See p120.

Silver Spurs Rodeo

Universal's CityWalk & Portofino Bay Boat Ride

By day, visitors stroll through this area of restaurants and shops on their way to Universal Studios and Islands of Adventure (see pp20–27). In the evening, CityWalk becomes it's own sparkling destination, a swinging Downtown with outdoor entertainment and pulsating crowds to rival Disney's BoardWalk. For 15 minutes of quiet romance, take the free boat ride (which runs until 2am) between CityWalk and the Portofino Bay Hotel (see p142). In the moonlight, the Portofino's faux Italian paint job looks even more convincing. Map T1

Swan Boats In Lake Eola

Tucked under the blossoming skyline of downtown Orlando, Lake Eola Park is a charming city oasis (see p52). Those seeking some (inexpensive) time alone can rent a two-person Swan Boat (propelled by pedal power) and cruise about on the lake. See p114.

Fort Wilderness Petting Farm

For kids who want to ride a pony (for a small charge) or get to pet miniature donkeys, goats, and other farmyard creatures, this splendid little park can't be beaten. Walt Disney World • Map F2 • 407-824-2900 • Open 8am–5:30pm daily • Free

Orlando Speedworld Speedway

This racetrack, 17 miles (30 km) east of Orlando, sees eight divisions of highly modified stock cars race each week. However, the most entertaining evenings are those with destructive, madcap races like Schoolbus Demolition Derbys, and Boat and Trailer Races. The price depends on what's on, but it's always a cheap night out. Highway 50 (at the 520 Cocoa cutoff), Bithlo • Map F1 • 407-568-1367 • Open from 8pm Fri • Adm • www.fascar.org

Left **Wet 'n Wild** Right **Discovery Cove**

🔟 Places to Cool Off

Wet 'n Wild
Orlando's best water park is full of rides and slides to keep the most hardened thrill-seeker's adrenalin pumping. But it's not all action – there are kids' rides and chill-out areas, too. See pp34–5.

Discovery Cove
Need to unwind on a tropical beach, swim with dolphins, or snorkel coral reefs? Well, if you check into Discovery Cove, you can. This exclusive (daily entry is limited to 1,000 people) and inspired Orlando attraction offers the features and personalized services of an upscale island resort. Admission is not cheap, but includes everything from lunch to wet suits and sun block. Reservations two months in advance are suggested. See p97.

Lakefront Park

Blizzard Beach
In the battle for water park supremacy, Wet 'n Wild's main competitor is this sizeable Disney park. It's what a ski resort would be like if it started to melt, with water slides replacing ski runs. Geared to teens and young adults, the park offers seven water slides and excellent rides, a wave pool, and kids' areas. If park capacity is reached early (as it often is), it closes to new admissions until later in the day. See p89.

Lakefront Park
In 2006, St. Cloud opened its renovated Lakefront Park. The nearly $10 million project includes a marina with 143 boat slips, a children's playground, picnic areas with pavilions and grills, a performing arts pavilion for concerts and special events, walking and biking trails, a white sand beach, beach volley ball courts and a water fountain playground, which has a great view of picturesque East Lake Tohopekaliga. See p108.

Typhoon Lagoon
This Disney water park is an enthralling mix of slides, tubes, and the largest wave pool in the US. It's well-suited to families with pre-teen children who'll appreciate the gentle nature of the attractions here. One stand-out is Shark Reef, a short snorkel course over a coral reef teeming with tropical fish and live sharks. Wannabe surfers (see p57) can pay an extra fee to use the wave pool out of regular hours. See p89.

Orlando Dive & Snorkel Tours
Dive at Florida's most spectacular crystal clear inland springs and rivers, which boast 200 ft (61 m) visibility and a wide variety of marine life. Swim with manatees,

For Sports & Outdoor Activities **See pp56–7**

turtles and catfish or enter the 'grand ballroom' 100 ft (30 m) below the surface in a cavern dive. Gear rental, transportation, and lessons are available. ◈ *13800 S.R. 535* • *Map G3* • *407-466-1668* • *Open daily* • *www.diveorlando.com*

Sammy Duvall's Watersports Centers

These Disney World-based centers were founded by four-time world champion water-skier Sammy Duvall. The Contemporary Resort branch offers parasailing, water-skiing, wake-boarding, knee-boarding, and tubing. Guests can either rent a boat and driver or take lessons. The slalom course is geared to more hardcore water-skiers. Guests can bring their own gear or rent it. ◈ *Map F1 & G2* • *407-939-0754* • *Open winter: 10am–5pm daily; summer: 8am–6pm daily* • *Adm* • *www.disneyworld.com*

Buena Vista Watersports

This friendly facility, which is home to Dave's Ski School, offers water-ski lessons, water-ski and wake-board charters, and rentals of personal watercraft (such as Waverunners and Seaddoos). The center, on the shores of Lake Bryan, is geared to beginners, and kids as young as three can join in. Non-skiers can use the lakeside beach, volleyball net, and picnic area.
◈ *13245 Lake Bryan Rd* • *Map G3* • *407-239-6939* • *Open 9.30am–6pm daily (weather permitting)* • *Adm* • *www.BVwatersports.com*

YMCA Aquatic Center

Lap swimmers who find hotel pools insufficient for training will delight in

Jet skiers, Buena Vista Watersports

this championship facility, with its 25-lane regulation lap pool. Although YMCAs are very family-friendly, the facilities here are geared toward serious swimmers. ◈ *8422 International Dr* • *Map T3* • *407-363-1911* • *Adm* • *www.ymca aquaticcenter.com*

Makinson Aquatic Center

On the eastern edge of Kissimmee, this center offers three pools – one for laps, one for kids, and another for the water slide. It's perfect for families with toddlers or youngsters for whom a major water park could be a bit overwhelming (and admission is far cheaper). ◈ *2204 Denn John Lane* • *Map H4* • *407-870-7665* • *Open Tue–Sun Mar–Sep (times vary)* • *Adm* • *www.kissimmeeparksandrec.com*

Following Pages **Discovery Cove**

Left **Canaveral National Seashore** Right **Turkey Lake Park**

Parks & Preserves

1 Canaveral National Seashore & Merritt Island National Wildlife Refuge

These two federal preserves bordering the Kennedy Space Center are home to scores of species, including endangered ones such as sea turtles, manatees, dolphins, alligators, bald eagles, and ospreys. Explore Canaveral's beaches (including a naturist one, Playalinda) and Merritt Island's trails, driving route, and observation deck *(see pp36–7)*. ◊ *Titusville • Off map • Seashore open at least 6am–6pm daily; refuge open at least 9am–5pm daily • Adm (seashore), free (refuge) • www.npca.org*

Lake Eola Park

2 Lake Eola Park

Burn a few calories on the 0.9-mile (1.4-km) trail that circles the lake here. Less energetic pursuits include feeding the birds and cruising Lake Eola in the swan-shaped rental boats *(see p47)*. This municipal park is also home to several annual and seasonal events, including the 4th of July fireworks show and the UCF-Shakespeare Festival *(see p64)*. See p114.

3 Wekiwa Springs State Park

These springs provide a fertile habitat for such species as white-tail deer, gray foxes, bobcats, raccoons, and black bears. They also provide some of the best places for paddling in a boat in central Florida. Canoe rentals, and picnic, grilling, camping, and volleyball areas are also available. ◊ *1800 Wekiwa Circle, Apopka • Map A3 • 407-884-2008 • Open 8am–sunset • Adm • www.floridastateparks.org/ wekiwasprings*

4 Lake Louisa State Park

You can fish, swim, or paddle a canoe, but you'll have to bring your own equipment. The beach has a bathhouse with showers, and there's a picnic area. White-tail deer, wild turkeys, marsh rabbits, opossums, and raccoons are common, and don't be surprised if a polecat (also known as a skunk!) cuts across your path. ◊ *State Park Dr, Clermont • Off map • 352-394-3969 • Open 8am–sunset • Adm • www.floridastateparks.org/lakelouisa*

5 Lake Kissimmee State Park

This park is one of the best bird-watching areas in the state. You might see bald eagles and snail kites, as well as whooping and sandhill cranes. Other residents include otters, wild turkeys, deer, and fox squirrels. On weekends, the park has a re-created 1876 cattle camp. ◊ *Camp Mack Rd, Lake Wales • Off map • 863-696-1112 • Open 7am–sunset • Adm • www.florida stateparks.org/lakekissimmee*

Turkey Lake Park

Unlike many state parks with spartan amenities, this 300-acre (120-ha) city retreat has a swimming pool, picnic pavilions, a lake full of fish, nature and jogging trails, three kid's playgrounds, and a farm-animal petting zoo. It also has camping areas if the call of the wild is too strong to leave. ◈ 3401 S. Hiawassee Rd • Map D3 • 407-299-5581 • Open 8am–5pm daily (to 7pm Apr–Oct) • Adm

Big Tree Park

The main pull here is the Senator, a 3,500-year-old bald cypress tree, a testament to the life-giving virtues of Central Florida's swamps. It is 17 ft (5 m) in diameter, 47 ft (14 m) in circumference and 125 ft (38 m) tall. The park has picnic tables and a boardwalk through the cypress swamp. ◈ General Hutchison Pkwy, Longwood • Off map • 407-665-2001 • Open 8am–sunset • Free

Tosohatchee State Reserve

Swamps dotted with hardwood hammocks (tree islands) and a 19-mile (30-km) stretch of the St. John's River combine to make this one of Central Florida's prettiest and most primitive parks. Photographers will appreciate the scenic locales, some with wild orchids and other flora. Hawks, eagles, fox squirrels, and songbirds can sometimes be seen from the park's trails. ◈ Christmas, 18 miles (29 km) NE of Orlando • Off map • 407-568-5893 • Open 8am–sunset • Adm

Wekiwa Springs State Park

Wheatley Park

This city park is more urban oasis than rustic countryside retreat. It features lots of facilities such as basketball, tennis, and sand volleyball courts, and picnic areas with grills for a barbecue. Kids will appreciate the well-equipped playground. ◈ 18th & Central Ave, Apopka • Off map • 407-886-1441 • Open sunrise–sunset • Free

Ralph V. Chisholm Park

This shady park, on the shore of East Lake Tohopekaliga, has various amenities including a beach, swimming area, horse trails, children's playground, softball and baseball fields, sand volleyball courts, and picnic areas. Bring your own equipment, food, and drinks. ◈ 4700 Chisholm Park Trail, St. Cloud • Off map • 407-343-7173 • Open sunrise–sunset • Free

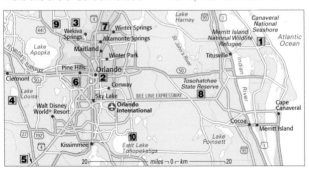

For more on day trips out of the city See pp82–5

Left **Clubhouse, Champions Gate** Right **Falcon's Fire**

🔟 Golf Courses

1 Disney's Osprey Ridge
Arguably the most challenging of Disney's five 18-hole courses, the Tom Fazio-designed Osprey Ridge features native woodlands, elevated tees, fairly large greens, nine water holes, and more than 70 bunkers. *Golf Digest's* "Places to Play" ranks it among Florida's best public and resort courses. (Max yds: 7,101 [6,493 m]. USGA rating: 74.4.) ⬧ *Golf View Dr • Map F2 • 407-938-4653 • www.disneyworld.com*

2 Grand Cypress Golf Club
Jack Nicklaus designed these highly rated 45 holes; the New Course was actually inspired by the Old Course at St. Andrews in Scotland. The club is semi-private with some public tee times. (Max yds: 6,906 [6,315 m]. USGA rating: 74.4.) ⬧ *1 N. Jacaranda • Map F2 • 407-239-4700 • www.grandcypress.com*

3 Disney's Eagle Pines
Pete Dye's Disney design challenges even the best golfers, with dish-shaped fairways, large sand traps, and pine straw rather

than grass in the roughs. Sixteen of the 18 holes have water hazards, due in part to the natural wetlands which line this course. (Max yds: 6,772 [6,192 m]. USGA rating: 72.3.) ⬧ *Golf View Dr • Map F2 • 407-938-4653 • www.disneyworld.com*

4 Disney's Magnolia
Here's a course with forgivingly wide fairways that let you hammer the ball. But don't get reckless: 11 of the 18 holes contain water and the course has 97 bunkers, with many waiting to gobble your miss hits. Part of the PGA's Funai Golf Classic *(see p57)* is played here. (Max yds: 7,190 [6,574 m]. USGA rating: 73.9.) ⬧ *Palm Dr • Map F1 • 407-938-4653 • Lessons available • www.disneyworld.com*

5 Celebration Golf Club
The father-and-son team of Robert Trent Jones, Sr. and Jr. came up with a course that has water on 17 of 18 holes thanks to natural wetlands, so bring an extra ration of balls. There's also a three-hole junior course for 5- to 9-year-olds. (Max yds: 6,786 [6,205 m]. USGA rating: 73.) ⬧ *701 Golf Park Dr • Map G2 • 407-566-4653 • Lessons available • www.celebrationgolf.com*

6 Champions Gate
Greg Norman created two 18-hole courses (the National and the International)

Villas of Grand Cypress

Make reservations at more than 40 Orlando-area golf courses with Tee Times USA 800-465-3356 or Florida Golfing 866-833-2663.

located in this resort community southwest of Disney, featuring woods, wetlands, and open land. Between them they have 13 water holes, and share double greens at the 4th and 16th holes. (Max yds: 7,048 [6,445 m] and 7,407 [6,773 m], respectively. USGA rating: 75.1 & 76.3.) ⊗ *1400 Masters Blvd • Map H1 • 407-787-4653 • Lessons available • www.championsgategolf.com*

Orlando Area Golf Course

Orange County National – Panther Lake

The elevation changes as much as 60 ft (18 m) in places on this 18-hole course, one of *Golf Digest's* top "Places to Play". It also gets high marks for course condition and pace of play. The course is surrounded by woodlands, while adjoining wetlands and lakes yield 13 water holes. (Max yds: 7,295 [6,670 m]. USGA rating: 75.7.) ⊗ *16301 Phil Ritson Way • Map E1 • 407-656-2626 • Lessons available • www.ocngolf.com*

Disney's Palm

This jewel of a course is surrounded by woodlands. Half of its holes have water,

and its 94 bunkers create headaches for those whose shots stray. The 18th hole is one of the toughest on the PGA Tour. (Max yds: 6,957 [6,391 m]. USGA rating: 73.) ⊗ *Palm Dr • Map F1 • 407-939-4653 • Lessons available • www.disneyworld.com*

Disney's Lake Buena Vista

This tight course with its heavily bunkered fairways and greens also uses dense pine forest to challenge golfers. Its most unusual feature is an island green on the seventh hole. Perennially rated as one of Florida's Top 20 in *Golfweek*. (Max yds: 6,819 [6,325 m]. USGA rating: 72.7.) ⊗ *Buena Vista Dr • Map F2 • 407-938-4653 • www.disneyworld.com*

Falcon's Fire

With just three water holes, the first nine may convince you to let your guard down, but seven of the last nine holes give you a chance to submerge a ball in two large lakes. This Rees Jones course opened in 1993 and hosts the Senior PGA Tour's qualifying school. (Max yds: 6,901 [6,310 m]. USGA rating: 72.5.) See p110.

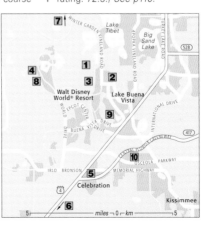

Left **Playing tennis, Grand Cypress Raquet Club** Right **Cycling along scenic country trails**

🔟 Sports & Outdoor Activities

1 Horseback Riding
Saddle up for 45-minute trail rides at Grand Cypress Resort's state-of-the-art equestrian center. There are horses suitable for all abilities of rider, and lessons are available in Western or English riding styles. *1 N. Jacaranda • Map F2 • 407-239-1938 • Open 9am–5pm daily • Adm • www.grandcypress.com*

Trail riding, Grand Cypress Resort

2 Tennis
Disney's Contemporary Resort has six hydrogrid courts and its Grand Floridian Resort & Spa has two clay ones. The nearby Grand Cypress Raquet Club has 12 courts, four of them all-weather. *Disney • Map F1 • 407-939-7529 • Open 9am–10pm daily • Adm* *Grand Cypress • 1 N. Jacaranda • Map F2 • 407-621-1991 • Open 8am–5pm daily • Adm*

3 Cycling
Get away on Disney's scenic bike trails. You can rent single, multi-speed, and kids' bikes at the Fort Wilderness Resort's Bike Barn. Tandems and cycles with baby seats and training wheels are also available. *Walt Disney World • Map F2 • 407-824-2900 • Open at least 9am–5pm daily • Adm*

4 NFL Experience
No matter if you're unfit or have never caught a forward pass. At Disney's Wide World of Sports, you can be a gridiron star for the day and take part in a program designed to make you an American football hero – minus the bruises and bleeding. *Walt Disney World • Map G2 • 407-828-3267 • Open 9:30am–5pm daily • Adm*

5 Swimming
Most of Orlando's hotels have their own pools, but for a change of scene and a place to swim serious lengths, try an aquatic center. *See p49.*

6 Boating
The man-made lakes around Walt Disney World are perfect for idling away an afternoon. Several of the resorts have small motor-boats and pontoon boats for hire. There are also paddle-boats for people who like a more rigorous work-out. *Map F1–G2 • Open at least 9am–5pm daily • Adm*

7 Watersports
Test your water-skiing legs at one of Sammy Duvall's Water Sports Centers (which also offers parasailing and wake-boarding). Buena Vista Watersports (which also charters and rents boats) is another option. *See p49.*

Surfing

In land-locked Orlando? You bet. According to the state's surf addicts, who sometimes rent the park after hours, Disney's Typhoon Lagoon *(see p48)* has wave-making down to a fine art. But you don't have to be a pro to give it a try. Carroll's Cocoa Beach Surfing School puts on a twice-weekly class for beginners. ✎ *Walt Disney World • Map G2 • 407-939-7873 • Open 6:45–9:30am Tue & Fri • Adm*

Fishing

Land your dinner (and a good fish story) with Pro Bass Guide Service, a Winter Garden outfit that specializes in guided bass-fishing. Local and regional trips to some of Central Florida's most picturesque rivers and lakes are on offer (pick-up can be arranged), as are offshore expeditions for saltwater species, such as redfish and sea trout. ✎ *407-877-9676 • Open daily • Adm*

Freshwater fishing, Central Florida

Hayrides

For something a little more unusual in the way of outdoor fun, try a 45-minute hay wagon ride around Disney's Fort Wilderness Resort. Expect some singing and dancing, and a good-time atmosphere that makes for a relaxing end to the day. One of Disney's most popular campground experiences. ✎ *Walt Disney World • Map G2 • 407-824-2900 • evenings daily • Adm*

Sporting Events

Florida Citrus Bowl

The annual college football showdown between the No. 2-ranked teams from the Southeastern and Big Ten conferences; preceded by a huge parade. ✎ *407-849-2020 • Jan 1*

Walt Disney World Marathon

A 26.2-mile (42.6-km) race with entrants from around the world. ✎ *407-824-4321 • Early Jan • www.disneyworld.com*

Speedweeks

Two weeks of motor action at Daytona Beach, ending with the Daytona 500. ✎ *866-761-7223 • Early Feb*

Silver Spurs Rodeo

Twice a year rodeo events for cowboys and girls in Kissimmee. ✎ *407-677-6336 • Oct • www.silverspursrodeo.com*

Bay Hill Invitational

Golf legend host, Arnie Palmer, plus players like Tiger Woods are the draw. ✎ *407-876-2888 • Mar*

Atlanta Braves Spring Training

Catch baseball's Braves in preseason training. ✎ *407-939-7712 • Mar • www.braves.com*

Orlando Predators

Grab a chance to support the local arena football team. ✎ *407-648-4444 • Apr–Aug*

Orlando Rays

See the local minor league baseball team in action. ✎ *407-939-4263 • Apr–Sep*

Orlando Magic

Don't miss the NBA team if it's the season. ✎ *407-896-2442 • Oct–Apr*

Funai Golf Classic

Disney hosts a multitude of tour professionals in a week of golfing events. ✎ *407-939-4653 • Mid-Oct*

→ *For more Orlando area events See pp64–5*

Left **Spa at Renaissance Orlando Resort** Right **Massageworks Day Spa & Fitness**

Spas

1 Spa at the Buena Vista Palace

Just around the corner from Disney's parks, the Buena Vista Palace offers an upscale experience that's from another world. This full-service, European-style spa has various styles of massage; body treatments (mud masks, wraps, and polishes); facials; and hydrotherapy treatments. It has steam rooms, saunas, and a health-and-fitness center. ◈ 1900 Buena Vista Dr • Map G2 • 407-827-2727 • Usually open 9am–6pm daily

2 Greenhouse Spa at the Portofino Bay Hotel

A state-of-the-art fitness center with a full-service spa (massages, saunas, facials, a couple's treatment room, and more) are on offer at this Universal resort. If you are a guest, you can choose to have your massage in your room. ◈ 5601 Universal Blvd • Map T1 • 407-503-1000 • Open 9am-6pm daily

Urban Spa at Eó Inn

3 Grand Floridian Spa & Health Club

The spa at Disney's Victorian-style resort has a whole range of services including water and massage therapies, aromatherapy, body wraps, and masks. There's a couple's treatment room and a well-equipped health club. The Grand Floridian also offers nutrition and fitness counseling. ◈ 4401 Floridian Way • Map F1 • 407-824-2332 • Open 8am–8pm daily

4 Canyon Ranch SpaClub at Gaylord Palms Resort

This spa has 25 start-of-the-art rooms for massage and body treatments including a Canyon Stone Massage, and a Mango Sugar Glo conditioning body scrub. There are men's and women's steam and sauna rooms as well as a relaxation room. ◈ 6000 W. Osceola Pkwy, Kissimmee • Map G3 • 407-586-0000 • Open at least 9am–5pm daily

5 Spa at Renaissance Orlando Resort

There's a full line of traditional spa services here, including massages (Swedish, deep tissue, and reflexology); body treatments (polishes and wraps); and a full line of facials, one of which is designed to introduce teenagers to the basics of skin care. In-room massages are available for an extra charge. ◈ 6677 Sea Harbor Dr • Map T5 • 407-351-5555 • Open 8am–8pm

6 Disney's Saratoga Springs Resort

The spa at this resort has a range of massage therapies (including hydromassage), body treatments, facials, pedicures and manicures. Treatments can be selected individually or as part of a full-day package, and the staff are happy to design personal treatment programs. Reservations must be made by phone in advance. ☉ *1920 Magnolia Dr • Map G2 • 407-827-4455 • Open 8am–8pm • www.relaxedyet.com*

Omni Orlando Resort

This beautiful resort, which was completed in 2004, has a first-class spa with state-of-the-art treatments and a deluxe fitness facility. From aromatherapy facials to sports massages, clients can take a break from the crowds at this luxurious secret resort and have a day of pampering. ☉ *1500 Masters Blvd, Championsgate • 407-390-6664 • www.omnihotels.com*

Urban Spa at Eó Inn

This is a funky spa in a downtown boutique hotel *(see p144).* Headliners include soothing Swedish, deep tissue, and Shiatsu massages; body waxes; seaweed or mud wraps; European, hydro-intensive, and men's facials; sea-salt scrubs; and a full line of salon services. Packages combine your choice of three to five services. ☉ *227 N. Eola Dr • Map P3 • 407-481-8485 • Open 9am–6pm daily • www.eoinn.com*

Massageworks Day Spa & Fitness

Located in a 100-year-old Kissimmee schoolhouse, this spa has an air of yesteryear. Treatments include massages (Swedish, neuromuscular, reflexology, and sports); therapies (salt scrubs, aroma steam, and mud-aloe); wraps (oil, marine algae, and sea clay); and colonic irrigation. Yoga, kick-boxing, and martial arts are also on offer, and there's a sauna.

Spa at the Buena Vista Palace

It's possible to combine treatments in three- to six-hour packages. ☉ *405 Church St • Map P2 • 407-932-0300 • Open 8am–7pm Mon–Sat*

Fawn Feather Spa and Salon

It's around a 30-minute drive from downtown Orlando, but if you're mobile, or staying in the north of the city, your reward is a soothing retreat. Services include massages (Swedish, prenatal, and aromatherapy); body wraps (mud, seaweed, and heat); and facials (European and anti-oxidant). ☉ *120 International Pkwy • Off map • 407-333-3571 • Open 9am–8pm Tue–Fri; 9am–5pm Sat • www.fawnfeatherspa.com*

Left **Exhibit, Mennello Museum of American Folk Art** Right **Orlando Science Center**

🔟 Museums

1 Orlando Museum of Art

Following a multi-million dollar makeover in 1997, the Orlando Museum of Art (OMA) has earned a reputation as one of the southeast's top arts museums. The fine permanent collection is dominated by pre-Columbian art and American artists such as Georgia O'Keefe, George Inness, and Robert Rauschenberg. These works are supplemented by touring exhibitions from major metropolitan museums, and numerous smaller shows of regional or local significance, although curators tend to avoid overtly controversial works. *See p113.*

2 Orlando Science Center

This huge, attention-grabbing, exploratorium-style museum boasts hundreds of interactive, child-friendly exhibits that are designed to introduce kids of all ages to the wonders of science. The center's four floors are divided into 10 themed zones. These deal with subjects ranging from mechanics to math, health and fitness to lasers, making this an educational and fun break from the usual Orlando theme park distractions. Don't miss the CineDome, which houses the planetarium and the world's largest Iwerks® theatre. *See p113.*

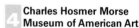

Detail, Charles Hosmer Morse Museum of American Art

3 Orange County Regional History Center

Given the region's relatively short history, this museum has wisely ignored geographic limitations. Exhibits not only feature local photographs and memorabilia, but a re-created Victorian parlor, a 1926 fire station, and fascinating temporary shows that cover themes relating to other parts of Florida, such as pirates and space travel. *See p113.*

4 Charles Hosmer Morse Museum of American Art

Here rests the world's most comprehensive collection of work by American artist Louis Comfort Tiffany, best known for his Art Nouveau stained-glass pieces. The museum's highlight is a spectacular chapel Tiffany made for the 1893 World's Columbian Exposition. There are also interesting collections of 19th- and 20th-century American paintings and jewelry. *See p119.*

5 Cornell Fine Arts Museum

Located on the campus of Rollins College, the small but stylish Cornell is Florida's oldest art collection. It showcases European and American paintings, sculpture, and decorative arts ranging from the Renaissance and Baroque periods to the 20th century. Among the highlights

Wells' Built Museum

are *Madonna and Child Enthroned* (c.1480) by Cosimo Rosselli, and *Reclining Figure* by Henry Moore (1982). *See p119*.

Mennello Museum of American Folk Art

This small, lakeside museum houses an unusual and charming collection of paintings by obscure curio-shop owner and Floridian folk artist, Earl Cunningham (1893–1977). In addition to his own work are traveling exhibitions featuring the works of other "outsider" artists. *See p113*.

Wells' Built Museum of African American History & Culture

Dr. William Monroe Wells, Orlando's first African-American physician, commissioned the construction of the Wells' Built Hotel in 1912 to provide lodgings for African-American performers. It was converted into a museum of Orlando's African-American communities in 1999. ✆ *511 W South St • Map P3 • 407-245-7535 • Open 9am–5pm Mon–Fri, Sat 10am–2pm • www.pastinc.org*

Albin Polasek Museum and Sculpture Gardens

Czech-American Polasek (1879–1965) was a sculptor who specialized in European figurative technique. In semi-retirement, he moved to this self-designed house and studio, where he continued working until his death. The beautiful gardens are filled with his sculptures, as are four galleries within the house, which also hold a few pieces from other artists. *See p119*.

Zora Neale Hurston National Museum of Fine Arts

Eatonville – the first incorporated African-American municipality in the USA – was the childhood home of Zora Neale Hurston (1903–1960), writer, anthropologist, and folklorist. This modest museum offers exhibitions centered on Hurston and the Eatonville of days gone by. *See p120*.

Maitland Historical & Telephone Museums

Artifacts, textiles, and photos from Maitland's pioneer days through to the heydays of the citrus and lumber industries are the focus here. In the same building, the Telephone Museum has vintage phones and memorabilia. ✆ *221 W. Packwood Ave • Map J4 • 407-644-2451 • Open 12–4pm Thu–Sun • Free (donation) • www.maitlandhistory.org*

Left **Orlando Philharmonic** Right **The Orlando-UCF Shakespeare Festival**

Cultural Venues & Organizations

1 Orlando-UCF Shakespeare Festival
This nationally recognized theater company has been performing the Bard's works since 1989. Their productions can be seen in three different Orlando locations. The company is best known for the annual spring festival *(see p64)* at Lake Eola Park, though it mounts high-quality performances all year. ◈ *407-447-1700 • Adm*

2 Orlando Repertoire Theatre
Founded as the Orlando Little Theatre in 1926, the Repertoire has grown into Orlando's version of a Broadway theater. It has three stages and puts on classic and contemporary plays alike. The year-round schedule is packed with high quality shows, but until renovations are complete, most are being staged at the University of Central Florida. ◈ *1001 E. Princeton St • Map M3 • 407-896-7365 • Adm*

3 Theatre Downtown
Recently named Orlando's Best Local Repertory Company, this volunteer organization has been producing first-rate shows since 1984. In 1989, it moved to a former appliance store, and in this casual setting has presented an array of classics, contemporary works (such as David Mamet's *American Buffalo*), and new plays by local writers. ◈ *2113 N. Orange Ave • Map M3 • 407-841-0083 • Adm • www.theatredowntown.net*

4 Enzian Theater
Central Florida's only full-time art-house cinema is a unique venue – its single-screen, 250-seat house is arranged like a dinner theater, with waiters serving food and drinks (including beer and wine). Featuring foreign and American independents, and with regular special-interest festivals, plus the Florida Film Festival *(see p65)*, this is a place for true cinephiles. *See p121.*

5 SAK Comedy Lab
A downtown favorite, SAK is Orlando's home of improvisation comedy. Shows are always funny and inventive, and there are two per night. The 8pm shows are usually family-friendly, while the later ones get a bit edgier, although obscene material is strictly avoided. Of particular interest are the series shows, such as *Foolish Hearts*, an ongoing, improvised soap opera. ◈ *380 W. Amelia St • Map P2 • 407-648-0001 • Adm • www.sak.com*

Orlando Ballet

Orlando Philharmonic

Orlando's resident orchestra boasts more than 80 conservatory-trained musicians. Venues vary, and include the Phil's home at Symphony Square, Leu Gardens (for outdoor concerts), and even SeaWorld. Its best-known showcase is the "Phil at Carr", an eight-concert series (Sep–May) at the Bob Carr Performing Arts Center, with guest artists in both classical and pop concerts. ◈ *Symphony Square, 812 E. Rollins St • Map M3 • 407-896-6700 • Adm • www.orlandophil.org*

Orlando Opera Company

This respected company has been producing opera since 1979. The season (Nov–Apr) is not long – four main shows for three dates each at the Bob Carr Performing Arts Center – but the quality of productions is high, with principle singers brought in from around the country and with music from the Orlando Phil. Smaller shows are also on offer at the Dr. Phillips Center. Ticket prices are very reasonable. ◈ *Dr. Phillips Center for Performing Arts, 1111 N. Orange Ave • Map N3 • 407-426-1700 • Adm*

Orlando Ballet

This small, but growing, company presents four major productions annually, including a version of *The Nutcracker*, choreographed by company artistic director, Fernando Bujones. Smaller shows are held on community stages, but the major productions are at the Bob Carr Performing Arts Centre. ◈ *1111 N. Orange Ave • Map P3 • 407-426-1739 • Adm • www.orlandoballet.org*

Osceola Center for the Arts

Kissimmee's home of high culture offers a theater, art gallery, and special events. The Osceola Center for the Arts (OCFTA) has an engagingly diverse schedule, eagerly offering a little bit of everything, from Broadway to Barbershop, storytelling to sculptures. ◈ *2411 E. Irlo Bronson Memorial Hwy • Map P3 • 407-846-6257 • Adm • www.OCFTA.com*

Mad Cow Theatre

A favorite among local actors, this burgeoning theatrical group has developed a reputation for small, high-quality shows. With a passion for both classic and contemporary productions, the theater represents the best from American and World literature. Past plays have ranged from Chekhov to Neil Simon. ◈ *105 S. Magnolia Ave • Map P3 • 407-297-8788 • Adm*

Orlando Opera Company

 For dinner shows **See pp80–81**

Left **Orlando International Fringe Festival** Right **Kissimmee Bluegrass Festival**

🔟 Festivals & Events

1 Renninger's Antique Extravaganzas

From Victorian furnishings to vintage political campaign buttons, you can find all things old and valuable sold at the 1,400 antique stalls spread across a meadow here. The prime goods go fast, so get here early (it opens around 9am). ◈ *Renningers Antique Center, Hwy 441 • Off map • 352-383-8393 • 3rd weekend of Jan, Feb, & Nov*

2 Kissimmee Bluegrass Festival

Poster, Florida Film Festival

Close harmonies, aching fiddles, and no drums – welcome to the world of bluegrass. Savor the sounds of American folk performers such as The Ramblin' Rose Band and The Osborne Brothers. Lawn chairs are encouraged and camping is available. ◈ *Silver Spurs Arena, 1875 E. Irlo Bronson Hwy • Map H5 • 321-697-3333 • 1st weekend of Mar*

3 Central Florida Fair

This massive 11-day shindig takes place close to Downtown Orlando, but its cowpoke attitude is a world away. The country-style attractions include carnival rides, livestock shows, country music, farming exhibits, and more fried food than you'll ever care to eat. ◈ *4603 W. Colonial Dr • Map C3 • 407-295-3247 • Early Mar • www.centralfloridafair.com*

4 Winter Park Sidewalk Arts Festival

For three days, this prestigious outdoor festival sees hundreds of artists exhibit on sidewalk stalls. Traffic comes to a standstill as the crowds mill around and ponder purchases. ◈ *Park Ave • Map K4 • 407-672-6390 • Mid-Mar • www.wpsaf.org*

5 Orlando-UCF Shakespeare Festival

The highlight of this troupes nine-month season is in spring, when they alternate two outdoor productions next to Lake Eola. One is staged traditionally, the other gets a modern twist. ◈ *Walt Disney Amphitheater, Lake Eola Park • Map P3 • 407-447-1700 • Late Mar–Early May • www.shakespearefest.com*

6 Orlando International Fringe Festival

With over 500 performances in 10 days, the Fringe offers improvised comedy, drag shows, stand-up, and more. Inspired by the Edinburgh festival, this premier event draws enthusiastic local crowds. ◈ *Various venues • 407-648-0077 • May • www.orlandofringe.org*

7 Zellwood Sweetcorn Festival

Eat as much sweetcorn as you can while listening to excellent country bands. A huge machine, Big Bertha, cooks up to 1,650 ears of corn every nine minutes. There are also some fairground rides and a crafts fair. ✪ *4253 Ponkan Rd • Off map • 407-886-0014 • Mid-May • www.zellwoodcornfestival.com*

Florida Film Festival
This 10-day festival is packed with more than 100 features, documentaries, and shorts. Filmmakers introduce their works, and a few Hollywood names make guest appearances. ✪ *Enzian Theater, 1300 S. Orlando Ave, and other venues • Map D4 • 407-629-1088 • Early Mar • www.floridafilmfestival.com*

Gay Days
Gay Days is a week-long blowout of parties and theme park visits for more than 130,000 gay and lesbian guests. By day, gay and straight mix in the parks; at night, parks and clubs are rented for evening raves. ✪ *Various venues • 888-942-9329 or 407-896-8431 • www.gaydays.com • Early Jun*

Anime Festival Orlando
This gathering of "Japanimation" fanatics has screenings, Japanese video games, dance and costume contests, and dozens of dealers offering hard-to-find collectibles. ✪ *Wyndham Orlando Resort • Map A5 • 3 days in Jun, Jul or Aug • www.animefestivalorlando.com*

Orlando-UCF Shakespeare Festival

Attraction Events

1 Mardi Gras at Universal
The ultimate 'Big Easy' party, with parades, music, and lots of beaded necklaces. ✪ *Universal Studios • Feb–Mar*

2 Disney Hollywood Studios Star Wars Weekends
Four consecutive weekends of Star Wars-inspired frolics. ✪ *Disney Hollywood Studios • May*

3 Night of Joy
A two-night showcase of contemporary Christian music. ✪ *Disney World • Early Sep*

4 Greater Gator Cookoff
An annual alligator-meat cooking competition. ✪ *Gatorland • Early Oct*

5 Halloween Horror Nights
Universal is transformed into a ghoulish home for the undead. ✪ *Universal Studios • Oct–Nov*

6 Epcot International Food & Wine Festival
Disney chefs and sommeliers strut their stuff. ✪ *Epcot • Oct–Nov*

7 ABC Super Soap Weekend
Fans meet and greet soap stars from ABC TV. ✪ *Disney Hollywood Studios • Early Nov*

8 Disney World Festival of the Masters
Daytime art exhibits and nighttime big-name jazz shows. ✪ *Downtown Disney • Nov*

9 Mickey's Very Merry Christmas Party
Evening seasonal fun complete with snow and enchanting parades. ✪ *Magic Kingdom • Dec*

10 Grinchmas
Enjoy a live performance of *How the Grinch Stole Christmas* at Seuss Landing. ✪ *Islands of Adventure • Dec*

Left **Downtown Disney Store** Right **Nike Factory Store, Prime Factory Outlet**

🔟 Places to Shop

1 Orlando Premium Outlets
This terrific 110-store complex is located just across I-4 from the east entrance of Disney World. It boasts high-end designer outlets by Versace, DKNY, and Barney's New York, as well as a mix of popular brands including Nike, Timberland, and Banana Republic. ⌾ *8200 Vineland Ave • Map F3 • 407-238-7787 • www.premiumoutlets.com*

2 Prime Factory Outlet
This branch of Prime is not only the largest and oldest factory outlet mall in Orlando, it's also one of the largest in the U.S.A. Located at the north end of I-Drive, the complex features more than 170 outlets in two fully enclosed malls and four annexes. The best stores focus on mid-line brands such as Nike, The Gap, Oshkosh B'Gosh, Puma, Dockers, Reebok, and Calvin Klein. ⌾ *5401 W. Oakridge Rd • Map U1 • 407-352-9611*

3 Prime Designer Outlet Centre
A third of a mile south of Outlet World is this 200,000-sq-ft (18,580-sq-m) strip mall offering nearly 50 decidedly upscale retailers. Fashion-conscious shoppers (both locals and tourists) flock here to cruise the well-stocked outlets of Brooks Brothers, Ann Taylor, Kenneth Cole, Saks Fifth Avenue, Fossil Watches, Coach, Nine West, Movado, and many others. ⌾ *5211 International Dr • Map U1 • 407-352-3632*

4 Florida Mall
Sure, it's a big enclosed suburban mall, but it's also one of the best in Central Florida and hugely popular with visitors and locals. Stores include Dillard's, JC Penney, Macy's, Saks Fifth Avenue, Sears, Nordstrom, Lord & Taylor, and more than 200 others. ⌾ *8001 S. Orange Blossom Trail • Map E4 • 407-851-6255 • www.simon.com*

Park Avenue

5 Park Avenue
This eight-block stretch of downtown Winter Park retains a times-gone-by quality. A canopy of live oak trees shades the brick-paved street, which is surrounded by low buildings and flanked by relaxing Central Park. Many of the stores on this upscale avenue are independents, but there are some national chains too, such as Williams & Sonoma and Banana Republic. There's no food court, but the sidewalks are lined with places for lunch or dinner. ⌾ *Park Ave bet Fairbanks Ave & Swoope Ave • Map L4*

Factory outlets – which sell last season's stock and imperfect goods at discounts of at least 30 per cent – generally open 9am–9pm daily.

Pointe Orlando

Pointe Orlando is a complex of shopping, dining, and entertainment venues. It offers something for everyone – a 21-screen cinema, a Wonderworks entertainment center, seven theme restaurants, plus more than 60 retail stores, including Victoria's Secret, Abercrombie & Fitch, and lots of specialty stores. The landscaped outdoor layout makes this a pleasant place for a shopping spree. ✪ *9101 International Dr • Map T4 • 407-248-2838 • www.pointeorlando.com*

Ivanhoe Row

Downtown Disney

There are two shopping options in Downtown Disney. On the glittery West Side is the massive Virgin Megastore, George's Guitar Gallery, and more than a dozen one-of-a kind shops. The more serene Marketplace is highlighted by World of Disney (the planet's largest Disney store) and the LEGO Imagination Center, a massive superstore. ✪ *Downtown Disney • Map F2 • 407-824-4321 • www.disneyworld.com*

Flea World

Claiming to be America's largest flea market, Sanford's Flea World is a Byzantine maze of more than 1,700 sales booths, which are bursting with bargains every weekend. The mostly new goods are already cheap, but you can haggle to lower prices still. In addition to an A to Z list of goods for sale, Flea World also has live bands, bingo, and an old-style amusement park, Fun World, for the kids. ✪ *4311 S. Hwy 17/92, Sanford • Off map • 407-330-1792 • Open 9am–6pm Fri–Sun*

Renninger's Antique & Flea Markets

Spread across a bucolic country meadow, Renninger's offers a large, folksy flea market, and a diverse indoor and outdoor antique market. The flea market offers everything from clothing to vinyl. The antique market has permanent dealers who specialize in excellent furnishings and jewelry. Renninger's also hosts the massive Antique Extravaganzas *(see p64)*. ✪ *20651 Hwy 441, 1 m (1.6 km) E. of Mount Dora • Off map • 1-352-383-8393*

Ivanhoe Row

This stretch of antique shops has thinned in recent years due to rising rents, but there are still more than a dozen stores offering vintage linens, clothing, jewelry, and various collectables. The period furniture available can range from Art Deco to Victorian. ✪ *North Orange Ave • Map N3*

Factory outlet stores often have sales at the same times of the year as regular shops (Mar–Apr and Aug–Oct).

Left **The Boheme** Right **Ran-Getsu of Tokyo**

🔟 High-End Restaurants

1 Victoria & Albert's
The high price can limit this to very special occasions, but trust the first-class food, fine wine, and faultless staff to make a memorable visit. It's decorated like Queen Victoria's dining room, and each table gets its very own Victoria and Albert as servers. Changing menus offer seven courses of international dishes, including apple-smoked Colorado bison and black bass with couscous. Take advantage of the wine-pairings (a glass with each of the five courses); it's cheaper and more varied than buying a bottle. *See p94.*

2 Primo
Housed in the sprawling J.W. Marriott Hotel, Primo has an elegant and warm dining area. Chef Melissa Kelly creates delicious dishes with Mediterranean accents using fresh local ingredients, including herbs and vegetables from the garden behind the hotel.

Emeril's of Orlando

Sit on the outdoor patio and sample the chargrilled Moulard duck for a special treat. ◈ *4040 Central Florida Pkwy • Map T6 • 407-393-4444 • Dinner only • No kids' menu • Pre-arrange vegetarian entrées • $$$$*

3 California Grill
The 15th-floor vista here gets top marks from both critics and diners (especially when the lights are dimmed for Magic Kingdom's nightly fireworks display), as does the Pacific Rim cuisine. Popular choices are seared grouper in a noodle bowl with ginger-crab salad, and pork tenderloin with polenta and mushrooms. There are also interesting vegetarian and sushi menus. It's hard to get a table on weekends. *See p94.*

4 Emeril's of Orlando
Famous US TV chef Emeril Lagasse owns this place, but only appears once a month, leaving the day-to-day cooking to his chefs. They create treats such as quail stuffed with Louisiana oyster dressing, andouille-crusted redfish, and a kosher salt and cracked black pepper rib-eye steak. This lofty place has a 12,000-bottle wine cellar. Book well in advance for dinner; there's a similar lunch menu at two-thirds of the price. ◈ *CityWalk • Map T1 • 407-224-2424 • $$$$$*

5 La Coquina
An imaginative beef, poultry, and seafood dinner menu makes La Coquina the most acclaimed of

Todd English's bluezoo

the Hyatt Regency's five eateries. The veal tenderloin with sake-glazed prawns, and the sugar cane-skewered scallops with rice grits and artichokes are two hits. Try the famous Sunday brunch, with its unlimited champagne and huge array of hot and cold dishes. ⊗ 1 Grand Cypress Blvd • Map F2 • 407-239-1234 • No kids' menu • Pre-arrange vegetarian entrées • $$$$$

Ran-Getsu of Tokyo

Sushi and sashimi are the big draw here. Try *tekka-don* (tender slices of tuna) or *una-ju* (grilled eel fillets), favorites of more adventurous diners. *Yosenabe,* a soup that blends seafood, chicken, and duck, is another popular choice. A Japanese drum group performs twice a night (Thu–Sat) and koi ponds and Japanese gardens outside help keep the mood peaceful. See p105.

The Boheme

The signature restaurant of the Westin Grand Bohemian Hotel is a key business venue and a prime romantic destination. Serving classic dishes with a modern twist, menu highlights range from Southern crab cakes to filet mignon and rack of lamb. Sip a Martini before dinner in the hip Bösendorfer Lounge. See p117.

Todd English's bluezoo

Celebrate the "blue zoo" of the ocean in a glass-accented dining room that feels like an underwater scene. Asian, Tuscan, and American touches appear in innovative dishes created with superb fish selections. Meat dishes are also available. ⊗ Dolphin Hotel, 1500 Epcot Resorts Blvd, Lake Buena Vista • Map G2 • 407-934-1111 • Dinner only • No kids' menu • Pre-arrange vegetarian entrées • $$$$

Park Plaza Gardens

For a touch of class, book a table at the exquisite Park Plaza Gardens. The glorious cuisine (such as blackened deep sea grouper with red lentils and curry vinaigrette) is enjoyed in a divine garden, much like a French court-yard. Take your pick from one of the best wine lists in Orlando, and finish off with towering desserts such as key lime pie. See p123.

Dux

An elegant, formal restaurant located in the Peabody Orlando Hotel (see p143) and which is named for the hotel's resident ducks. The menu includes superb seafood dishes, and the wine list is exceptional (just never ask for duck). ⊗ 9801 International Dr • Map T3 • 407-345-4550 • Dinner only • No kids' menu • $$$$$

Unless stated, all restaurants advise reservations, are non-smoking, take credit cards, and have DA, kids' menus, A/C, and vegetarian dishes.

69

Left **Outback Steakhouse** Right **Café Tu Tu Tango**

🔟 Family Restaurants

1 Rainforest Café

This jungle-themed restaurant provides noisy fun and a California-style menu. The mixed grill includes barbecued ribs, soy-ginger steak skewers, chicken breast, and peppered shrimp. Kids get their own special menu, the cartoon-like decor is good fun, and a "volcano" erupts every now and then. *See p95.*

Bergamo's

2 Romano's Macaroni Grill

Despite being part of a chain, Romano's has a neighborhood feel. The modestly priced Italian menu includes thin-crust pizzas cooked in a wood-burning oven, sauteed salmon scaloppini, and chicken marsala. Paper tablecloths and crayons will keep kids happy for hours. ⊛ *12148 Apopka-Vineland Rd • Map F2 • 407-239-6676 • $$$*

3 Coral Reef Restaurant

A 600,000-gallon (272,600-liter) floor-to-ceiling aquarium is a calming backdrop to this themed restaurant. Despite the high-brow, mainly fish and seafood menu, it's very child-friendly. Try the sauteed rock shrimp in a lemon cream sauce. *See p95.*

4 Outback Steakhouse

Tasty seared steaks are the headliners here; choose from rib-eyes, strips, fillets, and porter-houses. The Outback also serves good smoked ribs, shrimp and chicken over fettucine, rib-and-chicken combos, pork chops, and hamburgers. ⊛ *4845 S. Kirkman Rd • Map D3 • 407-292-5111 • $$$*

5 Restaurant Marrakesh

Mosaic tiles and a painted Moorish ceiling set the Moroccan scene. The food is flavorsome, with delights such as roast lamb *au jus* with couscous, and marinated beef shish kabobs. A belly dancer shimmies around and kids love to join her. *See p95.*

6 Café Tu Tu Tango

The menu in this lofty space is Spanish tapas in name but more international in flavor, with such diverse nibbles as baked goat's cheese, tuna sashimi, alligator bites, and snapper fingers. Performers (from sword eaters to artists at work) provide the entertainment. *See p105.*

7 Bergamo's

At this restaurant, the waiters sing Broadway tunes and opera while the chefs prepare the Italian menu. It covers all bases, with pasta, meat, and seafood – try the lobster, shrimp, clams, and mussels in a white wine and garlic sauce, or the veal T-bone

Unless stated, all restaurants advise reservations, are non-smoking, take credit cards, and have DA, kids' menus, A/C, and vegetarian dishes.

with olive and anchovy butter.
❧ The Mercado, 8445 International Dr
• Map T3 • 407-352-3805 • $$$$

Baja Burrito Kitchen
The draw here is the fresh and healthy Californian and Mexican cuisine, such as tacos, quesadillas, fajitas, and burritos, stuffed with lean meat and sour cream and cheese.
❧ 2716 E. Colonial Dr • Map N4 • 407-895-6112 • $$

Panera Bread
There are no preservatives in the dough used in the sandwiches and baked goods here available to eat in or take away; there's everything from whole-grain to focaccia and sourdough. Soup is also available. ❧ 7828 Sand Lake Rd
• Map F3 • 407-226-6992 • $

Chili's Grill & Bar
This international Tex-Mex chain serves scrumptious Cajun chicken sandwiches, margarita-grilled chicken topped with lime shrimp, and Cadillac fajitas with black beans and rice. See p105.

Chili's Grill & Bar

Dining with Disney & Universal Characters

1 Chef Mickey's
Mickey hosts American buffet breakfasts and dinners in the Contemporary Resort.

2 Restaurantosaurus
Donald Duck and pals host the Breakfastosaurus in the Animal Kingdom every morning.

3 Wonderland Tea Party
Every weekday at 1:30pm, Alice in Wonderland characters join guests in the Grand Floridian resort for tea and cakes.

4 1900 Park Fare
Have breakfast with Mary Poppins or a sit-down dinner with other Disney favorites at the Grand Floridian Resort.

5 Mickey's Backyard BBQ
Disney characters keep you entertained at this hoedown and all-you-can-eat American buffet dinner in Fort Wilderness.

6 Cinderella's Royal Table
A whole host of Disney characters join you for the "Once Upon a Time" breakfast in Magic Kingdom's Cinderella castle (park adm required).

7 Circus McGurkus
The Cat in the Hat, the Grinch, Thing One, and Thing Two turn up at Seuss Landing in Islands of Adventure at 2:45pm daily for a late lunch.

8 The Crystal Palace
Meet Pooh and his cohorts for American buffet breakfasts, lunches, and dinners in Magic Kingdom (park adm required).

9 Liberty Tree Tavern
Mickey and Goofy host the sit-down dinner "Liberate your Appetite" in the Magic Kingdom (park adm required).

10 Cape May Café
Join Goofy for a breakfast buffet at the Beach Club Resort.

For character meals, call seven days in advance (Disney: 407-939-3463; Universal: 407-363-8000). Expect to pay $ for kids, $$–$$$ for adults.

Left **Bar, Bar-B-Q Bar** Right **Downtown bar scene**

🔟 Places to Have a Drink

1 Lucky Leprechaun
A lively, welcoming Orlando institution. As its name suggests it has Irish connections and a friendly Irish flair. They offer a huge selection of great beers, including all the Irish beers you could hope for, and also food. There is karoke every night, live entertainment, and big-screen televisions showing all the important sporting events. Very popular hangout with the locals. *See p104.*

2 Independent Bar
A relaxed and hip place where you can dance to great tunes without the stuffiness of many other clubs. Fabulous mix of music from classic pop and hip hop to indie and jazz. Plenty of room at the long bar and on the spacious dance floor. *See p116.*

3 Cowboys Orlando
Kick up your heels at this popular country music dance venue, located near downtown Orlando. This huge club has four bar areas and state-of-the-art sound and lighting. It's open Thursday to Saturday to guests over 18 years old, and has nightly drink specials and dance contests. *See p116.*

4 The Bar at California Grill
This bar is a fabulous place to kick back, enjoy a bottle of wine and watch the fireworks over the Magic Kingdom. The secret is out, though, so come early for a table. Finding a spot at other times isn't too hard as long as you avoid the dinner rush. *See p94.*

5 Fiddler's Green
A big, noisy Irish pub, Fiddler's Green has an excellent beer selection, a homey, shabby ambience, and a bartender who pours faster than anyone in town. Darts and occasional live music form the entertainment, but people come here just to down a few beers and shoot the breeze. Lunch and dinner are served. *See p123.*

Bar-B-Q Bar

Most bars tend to open betweem 4–8pm and close around 2am.

6 Bar-B-Q Bar

It's little more than an average beer joint with sticky floors and loud crowds, but Bar-B-Q is *the* place to see and be seen for the more creative set. A favorite venue with local musicians, the bar gets packed whenever there's a good band on stage. People-watch clubbers cruising the Orange Avenue strip from a sidewalk table. ✆ 64 N. Orange Ave • Map P3 • 407-648-5441

7 Sky 60

Located above The Social (see p74), this rooftop bar is an Orange Avenue hotspot, attracting folks who prefer not to mingle with the masses but rather look down on them. Covered in whitewash, this airy spot is a classier option for folks who usually drink downstairs or at the Bar-B-Q Bar. Entertainment is typically provided via a DJ who leans toward refined, less aggressive grooves. See p116.

8 The Bösendorfer Lounge

Luxury is a tough sell Downtown, partly because the club crowd tends to be well under 30 and lacking serious funds. However, this swanky hotel bar is thriving, confirming that an older, upscale, and urbane crowd is more than willing to pay the price for a suave evening of fancy cocktails. See p74.

9 Dexter's of Thornton Park

A white-collar after-work crowd frequents this hugely popular bar/restaurant in a spacious, loft-like room. On fine nights, drinkers often head for the small outdoor space or spill out onto the sidewalk, jostling and juxtaposing with the folk from the fundamentalist church and a working-class beer joint that are located on the same street. Dexter's is also known for its great New American menu, and for serving lots of wines by the glass. There's another branch in Winter Park (see p122). ✆ 808 E. Washington St • Map P3 407-648-2777

Fiddler's Green

10 AKA Lounge

With more name changes than there are new moons, and an entrance that's tough to find (look for a doorway adjacent to the Pine Street Grill), it's a bit of a challenge to find your way into this bar. But the effort is well worth it, as this is one of Downtown's most comfortable and appealing drinking spots. The lounge occupies the top floors of two merged brownstones, offering plenty of space, a full bar, plenty of contemporary artwork, and a fine line-up of DJs and live bands. ✆ 68 E. Pine St • Map P3 • No DA • 407-839-3707

The minimum age requirement for drinkers in Florida is 21 years. Be sure to bring photo ID to avoid being turned away at the door.

Left **Hard Rock Live** right **Blue Martini**

Live Music Venues

The Social
The Social (formerly known as Sapphire) serves up an eclectic mix of live music. Sounds range from alternative rock to funk, jazz, and dance, with local DJs also gracing the club's legendary stage. For years, the club's policy of booking top national touring acts meant it was the shining light of Orlando's live music scene. Competition from much larger clubs is stiffer now, but this tiny spot, with its stylishly raw decor, remains O-Town's favorite venue to enjoy live music. *See p116.*

House of Blues
Wall-to-wall original folk art gives this giant venue a funky look. But like all things in the Disney empire, the decor hides a modern, smooth-running machine. HOB books amazing acts in every genre, from hip-hop to death-metal. Unlike many clubs, shows start and end on time, and the sound system is crystal clear. The one flaw is an incredible lack of seating with stage views, so be prepared to be on your feet all night. *See p93.*

Hard Rock Live
The ying to HOB's yang, Hard Rock has a more comfortable room, with balcony seating and good stage views. The grand ballroom decor is more appropriate for acts that want to perform in an elegant setting, so it's not surprising that top R&B artists such as Maxwell and Erykah Badu play here. The Hard Rock schedule is more erratic, with fewer top name bookings. *See p104.*

Blue Martini
They sell 29 different types of Martini here, of every color and description. This vibrant spot – they have live music every night – is popular with young professionals unwinding after work as well as at weekends. Tapas and a light meal menu are also on offer. The outdoor patio bar is a good place to mix and mingle. ◈ *4200 Conroy Rd • Map M3 • 407-447-2583*

The Bösendorfer Lounge
The lounge music craze that swept the nation a few years ago has almost vanished, leaving only serious practitioners. This elegant hotel bar is a swell place to sip cocktails and dig the duo in evening dress who sing near the $250,000 Bösendorfer Grand piano. Maybe it's the heavy drapes, the dark wood, or the well-tuned ennui of some patrons, but you feel wealthy just being here. *See p116.*

Blues Bar at House of Blues
Before it evolved into a chain of mega-clubs, the original HOB concept was closer to

Almost everyone needs to show ID to get into Orlando's clubs, most of which are for over 21's only; others set higher age limits.

this casual roadhouse place, which offers bayou-inspired eats, cold beer, and live blues bands on a low stage. Though they get little promotion, the bands booked here are excellent. And even if dinner prices are inflated (à la everything at Disney), the cover charge is zero. *See p46*.

Live music at the House of Blues

Adobe Gilas

The downside to Gilas is that they book mostly cover bands. The upside is a young, good-looking crowd getting smashed on tequila and dirty dancing with near strangers. The band usually sets up on the patio, but it's more fun and sweaty when it rains and the band crams itself into an inside corner. Sure, the southwestern theme decor gets old fast, but if you need to relive the days of dorm parties, this is the place to go. *See p104*.

Atlantic Dance Hall

Travel back in time to the glamorous dance halls of the 1930s and '40s and dance the night away! A great venue featuring wonderfully kitsch Art Deco interiors and grown-up entertainment, Atlantic Dance Hall is ideally located for those staying at a Disney resort. It hosts Latin bands playing live music Thursdays to Saturdays. Drinks can be pricey, but there is no cover charge. *See p93*.

Backstage at the Rosen Plaza

This swinging nightclub is located within the Rosen Plaza Hotel on International Drive.

Dance the night away to live bands and top DJs who play popular hits from the 1970s, the 1980s and the 1990s. Valet parking is also available. ◈ *Rosen Plaza Hotel, 9700 International Dr • Map F3 • 407-996-9700 • www.rosen plaza.com*

Bongo's Cuban Café

This lively venue combines Old Havana and Miami. In addition to delicious Cuban food, Bongo's serves up furious salsa rhythms on the sound system. There is multilevel indoor and outdoor seating, dancing every night, and great live music on Fridays and Saturdays. *See p93*.

Left **Tabu** Right **Downtown nightlife scene**

🔟 Hip Clubs

1 Hard Rock Live
Located at Universal's CityWalk, this vibrant and huge venue looks like a Roman Coliseum and offers seating for up to 2,000 people – great for a mildly decadent but definitely fun night out. The first floor has a standing-room only dance floor. Hard Rock Live's stunning sound systems are state of the art, as is its lighting technology. Emerging local musical performers, as well as big national and international touring acts, make regular appearances here. *See p104.*

Hard Rock Live

2 Tabu
Co-owned by one of the Backstreet Boys, this former theater is now a darkly stylish and cavernous club. The main floor boasts two large bars, a big dance floor, and video screens. Occasionally, the old upstairs balcony is transformed into a late-night sushi bar, and the lobby sometimes has a roster of supporting DJs. Lines can be long, especially when there's a big-name DJ or PA on. *See p116.*

3 The Club at Firestone
Once named top club in the US by *Rolling Stone* magazine, The Club occupies the interior of one of Orlando's oldest buildings. Its vast size, an awe-inspiring light and sound system, and an international DJ lineup still make this the best night out in Orlando. The Club attracts a mixed crowd that is very gay-friendly. The sounds run from trance to hip-hop to Latin, depending on the night of the week. *See p116.*

4 Revolution Nightclub
With more than 14,000 sq ft (1,300 sq m) of dancing space, multiple bars, and three separate rooms of music, Revolution is tailored for the alternative local crowd. Live bands and world-class DJs play Miami salsa, hip-hop, and techno until the early hours, while the Hydrate Video Bar area features giant video screens. 🌐 *375 S. Bumby Ave • Map D5 • 407-228-9900 • Adm*

5 Monkey Bar
A sign outside the Wall Street complex of bars and restaurants may proclaim the existence of Monkey Bar, but it takes a walk through the downstairs Tiki Bar and a ride on the elevator to enter this upstairs hideaway. Trendy and cozy, Monkey Bar offers food as well as quirky drinks and live music. Enjoy half-priced Martinis during happy hour (4–7pm Tue–Fri). 🌐 *19 N. Orange Ave • Map D4 • 407-849-0471 • Closed Sun, Mon • Adm*

Samba Room

This South Orlando club is upscale and hip. It's a restaurant during the week, but on Friday and Saturday nights it also has live Latin and Reggae music, and dancing until 2am. The menu features Latin fusion cuisine and there's also a cigar lounge. ✆ *7468 W. Sand Lake Rd • Map S3 • 407-226-0550 • Adm • www. sambaroom.net*

Antigua

Part of a sprawling five-bar complex, Antigua features a sleek multilevel design and caters to a beautiful – and noisy – crowd. Located in the heart of Downtown, this upscale club fills a section of historic Church Street with high energy. Dramatic waterfalls highlight four bars, three enticing VIP sections, and massive fish tanks. Women: 18+; men: 21+. ✆ *Church Street Station, 46 W. Church St • Map P2 • 407-649-4270 • www.churchstreetbars.com*

The Groove

The theme changes every night at this Universal CityWalk dance club, with music from the 1970s and '80s, current dance hits, Latin, techno, and more. The club area features a giant psychedelic dance floor, but the smaller areas – the Candle Room, Blue Room, and Red Room – are great for more intimate partying. The Groove is an attractive

alternative for teens, too, with dedicated teen nights on Mondays and Wednesdays. *See p104.*

The Social

This intimate live music venue is located in the heart of Downtown's party district. It regularly features big name acts and there's live music most nights. It also has one of the best Martini bars in town. *See p116.*

Roxy

Tucked into an after-dark desert area of town, Roxy is a big multi-floor dance club, with impressive hip-hop, Latin, and house DJs playing nightly. The loyal following tends to be less self-consciously trendy and more hetero than the usual Downtown club mix. For example, Monday Night Fights see amateur boxers from the crowd knock back a few beers then jump in a ring to fight each other. Well, the crowd *is* different from that found in Downtown. ✆ *740 Bennett Rd • Map N5 • 407-898-4004 • www.roxyorlando.com*

Roxy

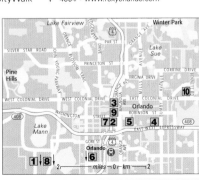

For more information on nightlife See pp72–5

Left **Wylde's** Right **Carmello, the Orlando drag queen diva**

🔟 Gay & Lesbian Hangouts

1 Parliament House Resort
Parliament is one of the southeast's premier gay resorts, boasting non-stop entertainment. Beside a 130-room hotel, there's a pulsating dance club, a piano bar, a country and western bar, a video bar, lakeside beach parties, and more. ⊗ 410 N. Orange Blossom Trail • Map P2 • 407-425-7571 • Free (Adm to club)

2 Southern Nights
Regularly named Orlando's best gay nightclub, this is a sizeable party hotspot on the weekends (Friday and Sunday for him, Saturday for her). Techno and house rule, except on Mondays, when it's Latin night. Drag shows and special events are always on the calendar. ⊗ 375 S. Bumby Ave • Map P4 • 407-898-0424 • Adm

3 Wylde's
Wylde's is a great place for gay men to enjoy an evening of lively entertainment and mixing and mingling. The club has many theme evenings, including a fun karaoke night and country music night. Men wearing underwear get happy hour prices for drinks. The club also has dancers, billiards and darts. ⊗ 3557 S. Orange Ave • Map Q3 • 407-852-0612

4 Full Moon Saloon
If your favorite Village Person was the Cowboy, the Full Moon is for you. It's a country and western club where hundreds of butch dudes in chaps and hats two-step their cares away. There's also a large contingent of manly leather types. The club is big, the outside space is huge, and it's considered a Sunday afternoon hot spot. ⊗ 500 N. Orange Blossom Trail • Map N2 • 407-648-8725 • Free

5 The Peacock Room
The Peacock's jazzy ambience is a welcome respite

The Peacock Room

from the thump of techno. This is a small, stylish lounge in the heart of Orlando's gay-friendly ViMi district. The decor is muted Art Deco and a small jazz band often plays. The cool vibe also attracts straights, making for a nice mix. ❧ 1321 N. Mills Ave • Map N4 • 407-228-0048 • Free

Savoy Orlando
A sophisticated North Orange lounge that caters for an upscale crowd of mostly professional gay men. High bar tables, black leather stools, and crystal chandeliers give the club a classy air. ❧ 1913 N. Orange Ave • Map P3 • 407-898-6766 • Free

Southern Nights

The Club at Firestone
Ensconced within a former Firestone garage, this giant venue has long been rated one of the southeast's top dance clubs, particularly with gays, ravers, and all types trendy. Although gay-only nights are gone, the Club continues to pump out house, hip-hop, and trance music for "the community." The upstairs Glass Chamber is a relaxing chill-out room with comfy couches. *See p116.*

Pulse
This is an Orlando hot spot for gays, with DJs spinning music from the 1970s and 80s. Tuesday night is Karaoke Night, while Wednesday is College Night. Hip-hop music is featured on Thursday nights, but whatever type of music you enjoy, you will find it here. This welcoming

establishment is a firm favorite for the Orlando gay crowd. ❧ 1912 S. Orange Ave • Map Q3 • 407-649-3888 • Adm

Faces
A long-time favorite for local lesbians, this homey place is busiest on weekends, when DJs up the tempo with house music. The bar staff's friendly vibe, plus pool, darts, and pinball, are other selling points. The first Saturday of each month is Latin night. ❧ 4910 Edgewater Dr • Map L1 • 407-291-7571 • Free

Studz Orlando
This popular high energy club welcomes both gays and straights. There's live entertainment, as well as pool, darts and karaoke nights. ❧ 1300 N Mills Ave • Map N4 • 407-898-0090 • Free

Left **Medieval Times** Right **Sleuth's Mystery Dinner Theatre**

🔟 Dinner Shows

1 Hoop-Dee-Doo Musical Revue

Book early for Disney's most popular "chow-and-cheer" night. The jokes are silly, the stars dress in costumes from Broadway's *Oklahoma!*, and if you don't join in the sing-along fun, the actors and audience will keep on at you until you do. Dinner is all-you-can-eat fried chicken and barbecue ribs; a vegetarian menu is available with 24 hours' notice. *See p93.*

2 Arabian Nights

Horses steal this show. Several breeds such as chiseled Arabians and muscular Belgians thunder through a performance that includes Wild West trick riding, chariot races, a little slapstick comedy, and bareback daredevilry. Horse fans can pet the four-legged stars after the show. ◈ 6225 W. Irlo Bronson Memorial Hwy • Map G2 • 407-239-9223 • 7:30pm nightly

3 Medieval Times

Horses take a secondary role at this spectacle. Instead, the action heroes are knights who get into sword fights, joust, and otherwise raise the roof while you feast on the likes of barbecued ribs, and roasted chicken with your fingers (after all, this is the 11th century). If you arrive early, you can tour a re-created medieval village. ◈ 4510 W. Irlo Bronson Memorial Hwy • Map G3 • 407-396-1518 • Show times vary

4 Spirit of Aloha Dinner Show

High-energy performers from Hawaii, New Zealand, and Tahiti show off their hula, ceremonial, and fire-dancing in an open-air theater. Meanwhile, tuck into the all-you-can-eat meal, which includes roast pork and chicken, fried rice, vegetables, and fruit. Learn how to make *leis* and do the hula in the pre-show. ◈ Disney's Polynesian Resort • Map F1 • 407-824-2000 • 5:15 & 8pm nightly

5 Pirates Dinner Adventure

The swashbuckling actors entertain with comedy, drama, and music, on a set that is is a full-size pirate ship on a water-filled "lagoon". The dinner buffet features roast chicken, braised beef, herbed rice, and more. After the show, there's a Buccaneer Bash

Arabian Nights

All shows charge admission, which sometimes varies depending on whether the performance is midweek or on the weekend.

Dance Party to help you burn a few of those spare calories. ⬥ 6400 Carrier Dr • Map U2 • 407-248-0590 • 7:45pm nightly

Makahiki Luau

A magnificent traditional Polynesian feast that celebrates people's co-existence with the earth and sea. This sumptuous celebration includes rhythmic music, Pacific Island dancers, authentic costumes, and delicious cuisine. The luau is one of the better meals on the Orlando dinner-show circuit. The show is inside the park, but theme-park admission is not required. ⬥ SeaWorld • Map T2 • 800-327-2424 or 407-363-2559 • Nightly • www.seaworldorlando.com

Sleuth's Mystery Dinner Theatre

The theater's cast stages eight different shows over the course of a month, all with a suspicious death and a twist before the mystery is uncovered. Meals include hors d'oeuvres before the show, then your choice of honey-glazed Cornish game hen, prime rib, or lasagna with side dishes, dessert, and unlimited beer, wine, and sodas. ⬥ 7508 Universal Blvd • Map T1 • 407-363-1985 • Show times vary

Capone's Dinner & Show

Settle into the 1930s and visit Al Capone's notorious speakeasy, a place where pseudo-mobsters and their molls entertain guests with a lot of song and dance. The all-you-can-eat buffet offers pasta, sausage with peppers and onions, baked chicken and ham, vegetables, potatoes, and whatever beer, wine, coffee, iced tea and sodas you care to drink.

Pirates Dinner Adventure

⬥ 4740 W. Irlo Bronson Memorial Hwy • Map G3 • 407-397-2378 • 8pm nightly

MurderWatch Mystery Theatre

In a twist on the normal murder mystery, the cast here acts out four possible endings to the story; the audience has to figure out which one is the correct plot. The crimes take place in a 19th-century-style restaurant, while guests partake of a buffet of prime rib, pasta, and more. ⬥ 1850 Hotel Plaza Blvd • Map G2 • 407-850-9555 • 6 & 9pm Sat

Starlight Theater

Broadway fans love this place, with songs by Rodgers & Hammerstein, George M. Cohan, and other legends. It's no rival to the London or New York stages, but it's a good show. A varied menu is on hand to feed the parts the songs can't reach. ⬥ 3376 Edgewater Dr • Map M2 • 407-843-6275 • 8pm Wed–Sat

There is no minimum age limit for dinner shows, although some may be unsuitable for younger children.

Left **Clearwater Beach, Gulf Coast** Right **Florida Aquarium**

🔟 Day Trips West

1 Busch Gardens
With five roller coasters, this park is a close second to Islands of Adventure *(see pp20–23)* on the thrill front. Roller coaster addicts rate the park's Kumba ride very highly. Busch Gardens is also a step ahead of Disney's Animal Kingdom *(see pp18–19)* when it comes to spotting nature's finest creatures, which are very visible here on the Serengeti Plain, Serengeti Safari Tour, and Rhino Rally ride. During summer don't miss cool rides like Congo River Rapids and Tanganyika Tidal Wave. ⊗ *3000 E. Busch Blvd, Tampa • 813-987-5082 • Open 9:30am–6pm daily • Adm*

Busch Gardens

2 Florida Aquarium
Florida's native species are just a fraction of the more than 10,000 animals and plants on display in this modern attraction. Wetlands, bays, coral reefs, and their creatures are featured in several galleries, and you can watch divers feed sharks and other marine creatures. ⊗ *701 Channelside Dr, Tampa • 813-273-4000 • Open 9:30am–5pm daily • Adm*

3 Lowry Park Zoo
Tampa's first zoo has 1,500 creatures, including Sumatran tigers, Persian leopards, and Komodo dragons. It also serves as a rehabilitation center for injured manatees *(see p31)* and as a sanctuary for Florida panthers and red wolves. A free-flight aviary and petting zoo provide a chance to touch some tamer species. ⊗ *7530 N. Blvd, Tampa • 813-932-0245 • Open 9:30am–5pm daily • Adm*

4 Ybor City/Centro Ybor
The Latin heart of Tampa contains the Ybor State Museum, plus trendy art galleries and lively cafés. Take the opportunity to try a Cuban sandwich, and strong *café cubano*, or to salsa and *merengue* into the small hours in one of the district's dozen or so clubs. ⊗ *Seventh Ave, Tampa • Off Map • www.ybor.org*

5 Florida International Museum
The museum's Kennedy Collection includes the rocking chair JFK used to soothe his ailing back, as well as full-scale re-creations of the White House's Oval Office and Rose Garden. Other draws are traveling exhibitions from major international collections. ⊗ *244 2nd Ave N., St Petersburg • 727-341-7900 • Open 9am–6pm Mon–Sat, noon–6pm Sun • Adm • www.floridamuseum.org*

The Gulf Beaches
6 Western Pinellas County has more than 30 miles (48 km) of white-sand, low-surf, warm-water beaches that are highly popular throughout the year. St. Pete Beach, Treasure Island, Madeira Beach, and Clearwater Beach are among the many headliners. ✆ *St. Pete Beach to Clearwater Beach • Off Map*

Historic Bok Sanctuary
7 This National Historic Landmark has nearly 250 acres (100 hectares) of gardens and grounds surrounding a 205-ft (62-m) bell tower and Mediterranean Revival mansion. The visitor center has a museum, video, café, and gift shop. ✆ *1151 Tower Blvd, Lake Wales • 863-676-1408 • Adm • Dis. access • www.boksanctuary.org*

Salvador Dali Museum
8 The world's most comprehensive collection of Salvador Dali's work from 1914 to 1970 can be found at this world-class museum, which opened in 1982. It has 95 oil paintings, more than 100 watercolors, and 1,300 graphics, sculptures and other works of art by the great Surrealist. ✆ *1000 3rd St, St Petersburg • 727-823-3767 • Open 9:30am–5:30pm Mon–Sat, noon–5:30pm Sun • Adm • Dis. access • www.salvadordalimuseum.org*

Caladesi Island State Park
9 This 3-mile (5-km) island, accessible by ferry from Honeymoon Island, is a lovely outdoor retreat traversed by a nature trail. A ban on cars helps keep it much as

Annie Pfeiffer Chapel, Florida Southern College

it was a century ago. In season, beach areas are dotted with the tracks of loggerhead turtles that nest here. ✆ *Ferry to island • 3 Causeway Blvd, Dunedin • 727-469-5918 • Ferry runs 10am–5pm daily • Adm • Off Map*

Florida Southern College
10 In the late 1930s, renowned architect Frank Lloyd Wright designed 12 campus buildings at this college – the world's largest collection. Highlights include the Annie Pfeiffer Chapel, the Roux Library, the Danforth Chapel, and the Esplanades. Pick up a walking-tour map from the visitor center. ✆ *111 Lake Hollingsworth Dr, Lakeland • 863-680-4110 • Visitors center open 11am–4pm Tue–Fri, 10am–2pm Sat, 2–4pm Sun • Free*

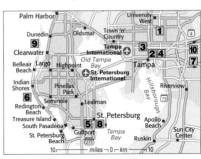

For Day Trips North & East **See pp84–5**

Left **Daytona Beach** Right **Ron Jon Surf Shop, Cocoa Beach**

TOP 10 Day Trips North & East

1 Kennedy Space Center

This well-conceived monument to America's space program impresses visitors with exhibits both mammoth, such as the Saturn V Rocket, and minuscule, such as antiquated space suits. Bus tours are a good way to take in the installations. *See pp38–41.*

2 Cocoa Beach

Just 60 miles (96 km) east of I-4 via the Bee Line Expressway, Cocoa Beach is the seashore closest to Orlando. The beach is picturesque, although the surrounding town is less so (apart from the lovely Cocoa Village near US Hwy 1). Surfing is taken seriously here, due in part to the presence of the Ron Jon Surf Shop, a vast surfing mecca that sells surf wear, beach gear, boards, and every imaginable beach accessory. ◎ *Off map*

3 Daytona Beach

During the annual "Spring Break," this legendary beach (just 90 minutes from Orlando along I-4) is the destination for thousands of vacationing college students, who drink and party until they drop. But sun and fun isn't all that's offered. Beach Street is lined with shops, restaurants, and clubs; and of course, there's the Daytona Speedway, home to the Daytona 500 and other NASCAR races (*see p57*). ◎ *Off map • Tourist info 386-255-0415*

4 New Smyrna Beach

Just south of Daytona Beach, New Smyrna is a smaller, calmer town that lacks Daytona's party scene. The white sand beach is picture perfect – but as at Daytona, cars share the space with sunworshipers. For food, the place to go is JB's Fish Camp, a raucous and friendly shack beside Mosquito Lagoon, which serves some of the state's tastiest fish, seafood, and key lime pie. ◎ *Off map*

Rivership Romance on St. John's River

5 Southern Cassadaga Spiritualist Camp

Buried deep in the woods near exit 54 off I-4, tiny Cassadaga was founded more than 100 years ago as a community of clairvoyants, mediums, and healers. Resident spiritualists promote the science, philosophy, and religion of Spiritualism; offer contacts with the deceased in the Spirit World; and provide a variety of healing services for the body, mind, and spirit. Staff at the Cassadaga Camp Bookstore can put visitors in touch with on-call mediums in the area and even provide a phone to make appointments.

Off map • Cassadaga Camp Bookstore, 1112 Stevens St • Open 10am–5:30pm Mon–Sat, noon–5:30pm Sun • 386-228-3171 • www.cassadaga.org

Manatee Seeker River Tour
These two-hour, pontoon-boat cruises specialize in safely allowing visitors a closer look at endangered manatees (see p33). Sightings of these gentle creatures are most frequent from late October to late March, but year round expect to see alligators, bald eagles, snakes, deer, and more. • Just west of Deland on Hwy 44 at the St. John's River • Off map • Tours at 10am, 12:30pm, 3pm daily • 386-917-0724 • Adm

Merritt Island National Wildlife Refuge
This 140,000-acre (56,000-ha) wildlife sanctuary (the second-largest in Florida) has more federally-endangered species than any other refuge in the United States. A six-mile (10-km) driving tour with shaded boardwalks weaves through lush pine and oak hammocks. See p52.

Rivership Romance
Operating out of historic Sanford, this 1946-built triple-decked boat offers daily "eco-dining" cruises along the scenic St. John's River. It's a truly civilized way to catch a glimpse of the Florida that tourists rarely see. • 433 N. Palmetto Ave • 407-321-5091 • Adm • No DA

Central Florida Zoological Park
Beneath this zoo's dense canopy of foliage, visitors can observe the residents (from howler monkeys

Local architecture, Mount Dora

to bald eagles, llamas, and zebu) at close quarters. Some areas fall short – the pacing big cats obviously need bigger cages – but on the whole, this makes for a rewarding trip. • 3755 N.W. Hwy 17–92, Lake Monroe • Off map • Open 9am–5pm daily • 407-323-4450 • Adm • www.centralfloridazoo.org

Mount Dora
Just 25 miles (40 km) from Orlando, charming Mount Dora seems plucked from the 1950s. The cozy downtown is unmarred by strip malls or chain stores. Instead, the local industry is antiques, with dozens of small shops on and around Donnelly Street as well as Reninger's Antique & Flea Markets (see p67) on the edge of town. Train buffs can enjoy a ride on the restored Cannonball, a 1913 steam engine, and Lake Dora offers plenty of boating opportunities. • Tourist info 1-352-383-2165 • Off map

AROUND
TOWN

ORLANDO'S TOP 10

Left **Lake Buena Vista** Right **Lake Buena Vista environs**

Walt Disney World® Resort & Lake Buena Vista

THERE WAS ONLY ONE *drawback to California's Disneyland, Walt Disney's first theme park, which opened in 1955: the area was prime real estate and there was no free space around the park in which to expand. So, following an aerial tour of Central Florida in 1965, Disney began covertly to buy large tracts of land. At the time, this patch of the Sunshine State was little more than cow pastures, citrus groves, and swamps, and was of little interest to anyone. Today, the 40-sq-mile (103-sq-km) Walt Disney World Resort is a self-contained and virtually self-governing entity (call 911 here and you get a Disney employee) containing four major theme parks, two water parks, several smaller attractions, and many hotels and resorts, which also spill over into the adjoining Lake Buena Vista area. For some of the 43 million guests who visit annually, it's a once-in-a-lifetime vacation, but many can't get enough of this enchanted fantasyland and return time and again to relive the experience.*

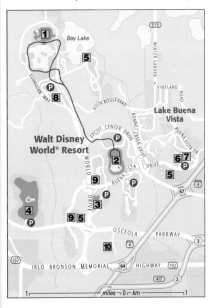

🔟 Sights

1. Magic Kingdom
2. Epcot
3. Disney Hollywood Studios
4. Disney's Animal Kingdom Park
5. Water Parks
6. Cirque du Soleil
7. DisneyQuest
8. Richard Petty Driving Experience
9. Fantasia Gardens & Winter Summerland Miniature Golf
10. Disney's Wide World of Sports

Magic Kingdom
Who's the leader of the theme-park pack? Disney's first Florida park is the most popular in the US. *See pp8–11.*

Epcot
Walt Disney's guys knew something had to appeal to curious adults and techno kids. Epcot is that something. *See pp12–15.*

Disney Hollywood Studios
A park that combines front-of-house fun with behind-the-scenes explanation. *See pp16–17.*

Disney's Animal Kingdom Park
Disney's fourth Orlando park is a place where elusive animals roam. *See pp18–19.*

Water Parks
Disney World has two water parks. The hugely popular Typhoon Lagoon, designed to resemble a beach resort devastated by a tropical storm, can hold more than 7,000 people at once, and has plenty of rides and attractions. Blizzard Beach's theme is a ski resort that melted and is a favorite among water slide fans. But whatever extreme weather they represent, these parks have similar features: long drops to build up speed and darkened tubes to confuse you before spilling you, laughing or screaming, into a wading pool below. The parks have seasonal opening hours, so call to check. *See p48.* ◊ Typhoon Lagoon • Map G2 • 407-560-4141 • Adm ◊ Blizzard Beach • Map G1• 407-560-3400 • Adm

Cirque du Soleil
Nowadays, circuses without animals are all the rage, and the Canadian company Cirque du Soleil is one of the best of its kind. So popular are its shows that, in addition to world tours, there are now permanent venues, too. Orlando's high-energy, 90-minute show, La Nouba, climaxes with a finale in which more than 70 performers execute an extraordinary trampoline routine. The ticket is quite pricey, but you're unlikely to be disappointed. ◊ Downtown Disney West Side • Map G2 • 407-939-7600 • Shows at 6 & 9pm Thu–Mon • Adm

Blizzard Beach

For information on Disney sights and attractions, including up-to-date hours of operation, call 407-934-7639.

89

Walt Disney

Walter Elias Disney was just 26 years old when his most famous cartoon character, Mickey Mouse, was introduced in the film *Steamboat Willie* (1928). Despite escalating success in the film world as he embraced first sound then technicolor, Disney had his sights set on more than just animation. He was the man who created the theme park, who envisaged as a kind of 3-D movie where each individual could spin his or her own story in a totally safe, controlled, and upbeat evironment. His first, California's Disneyland Park, was the perfect vehicle for bringing Disney's clean-living family values and nostalgia for tradition to the masses. It was also the only one of his parks that came to fruition before his death in 1966 from lung cancer, 11 years after it opened.

DisneyQuest

This interactive, indoor theme park is divided into four zones and entertains adults as much as it does kids. Highlights of the Explore Zone include Pirates of the Caribbean: Battle for Buccaneer Gold, and Aladdin's Magic Carpet Ride. The former puts you on the deck of a two-master schooner to play cat-and-mouse with foul-playing pirates and foul-smelling sea monsters. Aladdin's Magic Carpet involves wearing a virtual reality helmet and taking a ride through the 3-D Cave of Wonders in search of the genie. In the Score Zone, it's all about testing your game-playing skills. Don't miss the Extraterrestrial Alien Encounter where you get to fly a space ship and blast gigantic robots, or the Mighty Ducks Pinball Slam, a life-size, sure-fire hit for pinball fans. The Create Zone unleashes the designer within:

build your own roller coaster (and then ride it in a simulator), or take a short course in cartooning at the Animation Academy. The Replay Zone is filled with games where for an extra charge, you can win tickets that can be redeemed for prizes you can live without. Crowds are worse after lunch. ◈
Downtown Disney West Side • Map G2 • 407-828-4600 • Open 11:30am–10pm Sun–Thu, till midnight Fri, Sat • Adm

Richard Petty Driving Experience

Ever wanted to drive one of those souped-up, 600-horsepower NASCAR race cars, or even just be a co-pilot? Well, here's your chance to try for your dream – and a new land-speed record. The two-page waiver form that riders need to sign may shake your nerve, but there's nothing virtual about this attraction. There are two options: ride or drive. For the first, take the passenger seat while a professional drives off around the track at 145 mph (233 kmph); minimum age for this option is 16. Alternatively, spend a few hours or (if you have lots of cash to spare) days learning how to drive, and then race others for up to 30 laps (minimum age is 18 years). ◈ *Walt Disney World Speedway • Map F1 • 800-237-3889 • Opening times vary • Adm*

Fantasia Gardens & Winter Summerland Miniature Golf

Orlando in general and Walt Disney World Resort in particular have some great golf courses *(see pp54–5)*, but not everyone likes to take the game so seriously, or has the makings of a pro. These two miniature golf courses offer a total of 72 holes of putting fun. Inspired by the classic Disney cartoon, *Fantasia*, Fantasia Gardens'

Richard Petty Driving Experience

18 holes have an animal theme. Located near Disney Hollywood Studios, it's the more forgiving of the two courses, and so the best choice for young kids or beginners. Winter Summerland is a scale model of a large course, complete with bunkers, water hazards, frustrating putting greens, and holes that are up to 75 ft (23 m) long. Choose between the winter and summer themed courses. ❂ *Fantasia Gardens • Map G2 • 407-560-4582 • Open 10am–11pm daily • Adm* ❂ *Winter Summerland • Map G1 • 407-560-3000 • Open 10am–11pm daily • Adm*

10 Disney's Wide World of Sports

Disney's sports complex is the spring training home of Major League baseball's Atlanta Braves (Feb–Mar) and minor league baseball's Orlando Rays, a farm team for the Tampa Bay Devil Rays (Apr–Sep). It's also a winter home for basketball's Harlem Globetrotters. Other facilities in the 200-acre (80-ha) complex, which is used for all kinds of amateur sports and athletics,

include: a fitness center; basketball, volleyball, and tennis courts; softball, soccer, and lacrosse fields; a martial-arts venue; and a golf-driving range. Disney's Wide World of Sports is also the home of the NFL Experience *(see p56)*. There is an extreme sports area catering for skateboarders, in-line skaters, and cyclists, which is now open for special events. ❂ *Map G2 • 407-939-1500 • Opening times vary • Adm*

Hidden Mickeys

Hidden Mickeys started many years ago as a joke among park designers. Today they're a Disney tradition. They're images of the world's most famous mouse: silhouettes of Mickey's ears, his head and ears or his whole body, semi-hidden throughout the parks and resorts. They can be anywhere: in the landscaping, in the murals you pass while waiting in ride lines, and even overhead, for example on the Earffel Tower in Disney Hollywood Studios. See how many you can spot (www.hiddenmickeys.org).

For more on sports and activities **See pp56–7**

Disney's BoardWalk

Best Shops

1 Yong Feng Shangdian Department Store

Here's an excellent source for all things Asian, from jade figurines to silk robes, and inlaid mother-of-pearl furnishings to wind chimes. ✆ *China Pavilion, World Showcase, Epcot • Map G2 • Adm*

2 Berber Oasis

Hand-tied Berber rugs, camel-bone boxes, and more are on offer in this square, which has the bustle but not the hustle of the real thing. ✆ *Morocco Pavilion, World Showcase, Epcot • Map G2 • Adm*

3 LEGO Imagination Center

Kids love the play area, which has enough LEGO pieces to build almost anything. Inside, the cash registers sing as parents buy the latest Lego gadgets. ✆ *Downtown Disney Marketplace • Map G2*

4 Mitsukoshi Department Store

An amazing selection of kimonos, samurai swords, bonsais, Japanese Disneyana, and kites is sold here. ✆ *Japan Pavilion, World Showcase, Epcot • Map G2 • Adm*

5 Guitar Gallery

This showroom is crammed with 150 models of guitar (including one made of rosewood and ivory costing $25,000), catering to all budgets. ✆ *Downtown Disney West Side • Map G2*

6 Virgin Megastore

Listen to recent releases at the numerous sound stations in this store, or browse for videos and books. ✆ *Downtown Disney West Side • Map G2*

7 Art of Disney

This large gallery is one of a kind in Florida. You'll find Disney sculptures, animation cels, and other collectibles. ✆ *Downtown Disney Marketplace • Map G2*

8 Hoypoloi Gallery

This small but sensory gallery sells sculptures, ceramics, and other imaginative oddities made of metal, stone, clay, and wood. ✆ *Downtown Disney West Side • Map G2*

9 Mickey's Mart

Everything in this shop located between Disney Tails and Disney at Home is $10 or less. Every week there is a featured sale item. ✆ *Downtown Disney Marketplace • Map G2*

10 World of Disney

The folks at Disney claim this store has the largest and most unique collection of Disney character merchandise on the planet. If you're a hardcore Disney fanatic, it's easy to spend a small fortune here. ✆ *Downtown Disney Marketplace • Map G2*

Forget to buy something? Call 407-363-6200, give the item's description and where you saw it. You can probably order it by phone.

Downtown Disney

🔟 Nighttime Attractions

House of Blues
One of Orlando's best venues for live music with a wide variety of musical acts. *See p74.* ✪ *Downtown Disney West Side • Map G2 • 407-934-2583 • Adm*

Disney's BoardWalk
By night, this "seaside" boardwalk is thronged with guests enjoying the buzzing vibe and some great restaurants and clubs. *See p46.* ✪ *Map G2 • Free*

Downtown Disney
Probably Disney's best spot for night owls, with lots of bars and clubs to choose from. *See p46.* ✪ *Map G2 • Free to walk around*

Cirque du Soleil
In a tent-like theater in Disney's West Side, this avant-garde circus troupe spotlights superhuman acrobats. *See p89.*

DisneyQuest
Heaven for video gamers, here kids can design their own roller coaster and ride it, or steer a ship in Pirates of the Caribbean. *See p90.*

Bongo's Cuban Café
This venue evokes images of Havana of the 1940s and '50s, and has live music at weekends. *See p75.* ✪ *Downtown Disney, 1498 E. Buena Vista Dr • Map G2 • 407-828-0999 • Adm on Sat*

ESPN Club
Watch big games on a giant screen, play arcade games, and join the audience for live shows at this sports bar, which serves burgers and steaks. ✪ *2101 Epcot Resorts Blvd • Map G2 • 407-939-1177*

Hoop-Dee-Doo Musical Revue
This family show combines an all-you-can-eat dinner with country & western dancing, singing, and comedy. Unlimited draft beer, wine, and soft drinks are included. *See p80.* ✪ *Disney's Fort Wilderness Resort • Map F1 • 407-WDW- DINE • 5, 7:15 & 9:30pm nightly*

Atlantic Dance Hall
This glorious 1930s-style dance hall has been re-imagined as a predominantly Latin hotspot, with a live Latin band (Thu–Sat) and a Latin DJ who spins tunes (Tue). *See p75.* ✪ *Disney's BoardWalk • Map G2 • Closed Sun & Mon • Adm*

Chip 'n' Dale's Campfire Sing-A-Long
Enjoy songs and marshmallows around a campfire, followed by a different Disney movie every night. It is open to all – just park at the River Country entrance and take the bus to the party. ✪ *Meadow Trading Post, Fort Wilderness Campground • Map G2 • 407-824-2900 • Free • 8pm (summer), 7pm (rest of the year)*

Guests must be 21 or over to get into clubs and bars in Orlando, and need to have picture ID (driving license or passport) to prove it.

California Grill

🔟 Resort Area Restaurants

1 Victoria & Albert's

This romantic gem has an international menu that is served by staff dressed as Victoria and Albert. *See p68.* ✪ *Disney's Grand Floridian Resort & Spa • Map F1 • 407-824-1089 • Pre-arrange vegetarian entrées • No kids' menu • $$$$$*

2 California Grill

This vegetarian-friendly restaurant offers delicious California cuisine in a romantic 15th-floor space. *See p68.* ✪ *Disney's Contemporary Resort • Map F1 • 407-824-1576 • $$$$*

3 Dragon Court Chinese Buffet

For those who love Chinese food head for this no-frills buffet restaurant and its huge selection of dishes. ✪ *12384 Apopka-Vineland Rd • Map F2 • 407-238-9996 • $*

4 Jiko – The Cooking Place

This restaurant features a show kitchen and an inventive menu: banana-leaf steamed sea bass is a typical dish. ✪ *Disney's Animal Kingdom Lodge • Map G1 • 407-938-3000 • $$$$*

5 Artist Point

Bison rib-eye steak and nut-and-herb crusted lamb chops are a few of the delicious options here. There's patio dining as well. ✪ *Disney's Wilderness Lodge • Map F1 • 407-824-3200 • $$$$*

6 Emeril's Tchoup Chop

The Polynesian fare here has a New Orleans twist. Menu highlights include dumplings and pot stickers followed by fish cooked in clay pots, and Kona-glazed duck. ✪ *Royal Pacific Resort, 6300 Hollywood Way • Map T2 • 407-503-2467 • No kids' menu • $$$$*

7 Sanaa

The Indian-spiced African menu here is loaded with slow-cooked delights, grilled over a wood fire or roasted in a tandoor oven. ✪ *Disney's Animal Kingdom Lodge • Map G1 • 407-WDW-DINE • $$$$*

8 Columbia Restaurant Celebration

Come here for a taste of old Havana. Indulge in crab-stuffed pompano or dive into the exquisite calamari. ✪ *649 Front St • Map G2 • 407-566-1505 • $$$*

9 Wolfgang Puck's Café

Grilled pizza, spicy tuna rolls, and pumpkin risotto are some of the eclectic options made here by the acclaimed California chef. ✪ *Downtown Disney West Side • Map G2 • 407-938-9653 • $$$$*

10 Portobello Yacht Club Restaurant

This classy eatery is sure to please with thin crust pizzas, pastas, and Italian food such as slow-roasted pork loin. ✪ *Downtown Disney • Map G2 • 407-934-8888 • $$$$$*

Unless stated, all restaurants advise reservations, are non-smoking, take credit cards, and have DA, kids' menus, A/C, and vegetarian dishes.

Price Categories
For a three-course meal for one, a glass of house wine, and all unavoidable extra charges including tax.

$	under $20
$$	$20–$30
$$$	$30–$45
$$$$	$45–$60
$$$$$	over $60

Coral Reef

🔟 Theme Park Restaurants

Around Walt Disney World Resort & Lake Buena Vista

Marrakesh
The seafood *bastilla* (pastry filled with fish, shrimp, mushroom, vermicelli, onion, and egg) is heavenly. Garlicky lemon chicken ranks a close second. 🅂 *Morocco Pavilion, Epcot • Map G2 • 407-939-3463 • $$$$*

Rainforest Café
American cuisine inspired by Mexican, Carribean, and Asian flavors is served in an indoor rainforest setting. If you don't like volume and kids, this isn't for you. 🅂 *Disney's Animal Kingdom • Map G1 • 407-939-3463 • Park adm not required • $$$$*

Coral Reef
Classical music and aquarium visuals are the setting here. Try the roasted snapper with veggies. 🅂 *Living Seas Pavilion, Epcot • Map G2 • 407-939-3463 • $$$$*

Cinderella's Royal Table
This restaurant in a castle has a great menu, with tasty prime-rib pastry-pie leading the way. 🅂 *Fantasyland, Magic Kingdom • Map F1 • 407-939-3463 • Pre-arrange vegetarian entrées • No alcohol • $$$$*

Akershus
Hunker down for traditional Norweigian dishes (herring, potato salad, gravlax in mustard sauce, venison stew, and more) in a medieval castle setting. 🅂 *Norway Pavilion, Epcot • Map G2 • 407-939-3463 • $$$*

Hollywood Brown Derby
Polish off SoCal dishes such as skillet-seared tuna with the signature grapefruit cake with cream-cheese icing. 🅂 *Disney Hollywood Studios • Map G2 • 407-939-3463 • Pre-arrange vegetarian entrées • $$$$*

San Angel Inn
Try *mole poblano* (chicken with spices and chocolate) or beef with black beans and fried plantain at this south-of-the-border eatery. 🅂 *Mexico Pavilion, Epcot • Map G2 • 407-939-3463 • $$$*

Rose & Crown Pub & Dining Room
A pub-grub joint offering British staples such as bangers and mash, rib with Yorkshire pudding, and Cornish pasties. 🅂 *UK Pavilion, Epcot • Map G2 • 407-939-3463 • Pre-arrange vegetarian entrées • $$$*

Chefs de France
Three French chefs created this brasserie-style restaurant full of Gallic flare and flavor. 🅂 *France Pavilion, Epcot • Map G2 • 407-939-3463 • Pre-arrange vegetarian entrées • $$$$*

Liberty Tree Tavern
Buffet-style American fare, such as roasted turkey, flank steak, and ham, is served in a colonial setting. 🅂 *Liberty Sq, Magic Kingdom • Map F1 • 407-939-3463 • Pre-arrange vegetarian entrées • No alcohol • $$$*

For information on Priority Seating in Walt Disney World Resort See p134

Left **Wet 'n Wild** Right **Universal Studios**

International Drive Area

CONSIDERED THE TIMES SQUARE OF *Orlando, International Drive is a brash* 10-mile (16-km) strip boasting five theme parks, countless attractions open day and night, including Universal's CityWalk entertainment complex, and the USA's second-largest convention center. Added to the mix are hundreds of hotels and resorts catering to all budgets, shopping malls and outlet stores, and themed and fast-food restaurants. As a package, the result is a frenetic zone, which, despite its wall-to-wall neon signs and visual overload, has become a serious competitor of Disney World, appealing to visitors who prefer to stay away from the clutches of Mickey but want to be in the thick of the action.

CityWalk, Universal Orlando

Sights & Attractions

1. Islands of Adventure
2. Universal Studios Florida
3. Wet 'n Wild
4. SeaWorld Orlando
5. Discovery Cove
6. Fun Spot Action Park
7. Ripley's Believe It or Not! Odditorium
8. The Holy Land Experience
9. WonderWorks
10. Titanic – The Experience

Islands of Adventure

Islands of Adventure
Few visitors would contest the claim of this Universal park to being king of the Orlando thrill-ride circuit. *See pp20–23.*

Universal Studios Florida
Part studio and part attraction, the movie-themed rides and shows here really let visitors step inside the movies. *See pp24–7.*

Wet 'n Wild
It's hard to out-do Disney, but Wet 'n Wild is arguably Orlando's best sun-and-swim water park attraction, with plenty of slides and rides to amuse. *See pp34–5.*

SeaWorld Orlando
Anheuser-Busch's Orlando outpost offers animal attractions and a refreshing change of pace to the fast rides and cartoon characters overrunning the other parks. *See pp28–31.*

Discovery Cove
You might be in land-locked Orlando, but you can still fulfil those tropical island fantasies of swimming with dolphins and snorkeling over coral reefs if you check in to Discovery Cove. The dolphin swim is the biggest draw (each session lasts about one hour), but the white-sand beaches, snorkeling opportunities in fresh and

salt-water lagoons, and soothing beach-resort vibe elicits just as much praise. Admission is not cheap (largely because there are never more than 1,000 visitors daily), but you get almost everything you need for the day thrown in, including sun block, lunch, and snorkel gear, as well as a seven-day pass to SeaWorld. This secluded oasis is not for everyone – kids might miss the lack of thrill rides – but for a unique beach escape that doesn't require leaving Orlando, this is the place. *See p48.* ◎ *6000 Discovery Cove Way • Map T6 • 407-370-1280 • Open 9am–5:30pm daily • Adm*

Discovery Cove

Fun Spot Action Park
This arcade-cum-amusement-park has something for everyone who has a little bit of the child in them. The park has four go-kart tracks, with corkscrew and banked turns, 30-degree descents, bridges, and more. In addition, there are bumper boats and cars, a 100-ft (30-m) Ferris wheel, 100 arcade games, and a kid zone that has swings, a train, spinning tea cups, and flying bears. *See p44.* ◎ *5551 Del Verde Way, Orlando • Map U2 • 407-363-3867 • noon–11pm Mon–Fri, 10am–11pm Sat–Sun • Free (but ride and game prices vary) • Min age for solo go-karting is 10 yrs*

Fun Spot Action Park

Ripley's Believe It or Not! Odditorium

7 Ripley's Believe It or Not! Odditorium

If you're a fan of the bizarre, you'll love Ripley's. This worldwide chain of attractions displays the unbelievable finds of Robert Ripley's 40 years of adventures, the reports of which were published in more than 300 newspapers and read by more than 80 million people. The Orlando branch has a full-scale model of a 1907 Silver Ghost Rolls Royce (with moving engine parts) built out of 1,016,711 match sticks and 63 pints (36 l) of glue; a flute made of human bones; a mosaic of the Mona Lisa made out of toast; shrunken heads; a five-legged cow; and a portrait of Van Gogh made from 3,000 postcards. You'll also encounter a holographic 1,069-lb- (485-kg) man, plus films of strange feats such as people swallowing coat-hangers. *See p44.* **✪** *8201 International Dr • Map T3 • 407-363-4418 • Open 9–1am daily • Adm*

The Peabody Ducks

Their existence came about because of a practical joke, but now these five mallards, which reside in the Peabody Hotel *(see p143)*, are among the best known and most unusual celebreties in I-Drive. As befits VIPs (Very Important Poultry), they spend much of each day in their $100,000 glass-enclosed home, called the 'Duck Palace.' But what draws the crowds is their twice daily procession (at 11am and 5pm), when they waddle through the hotel lobby, led by their own red-coated duck master, on the way to and from the lobby fountain.

8 The Holy Land Experience

Marvin J. Rosenthal, a Christian convert and Baptist minister, created quite a stir when he opened this religious theme park in 2001. Set in a half-scale reconstruction of the Temple of the Great King, which stood in Jerusalem in the 1st century AD, the park aims to take visitors 7,000 miles (11,200 km) away and 3,000 years back to the ancient Jerusalem of biblical times (BC 1450 to AD 66 to be exact). The attraction has models of the limestone caves where the Dead Sea Scrolls were discovered and Jesus's tomb. It also has displays of rare antiquated Bibles and biblical manuscripts, an outdoor stage where actors portraying biblical personalities tell stories from the Old and New Testaments, and a café that serves Middle Eastern food. *See p44.* **✪** *4655 Vineland Rd • Map D4 • 407-872-2272 • Open 10am–7pm, sometimes later, Mon–Sat; noon–6pm Sun • Adm*

The Holy Land Experience

WonderWorks

You can't miss this attraction from the outside: it looks as though a classical building has landed upside down on top of a warehouse. Inside, there are 85 hands-on exhibits. Highlights include an earthquake simulator; a Bridge of Fire, where you can

WonderWorks

literally experience the hair-raising effects of 250,000 watts of static electricity; and Virtual Hoops, which uses some of the latest cinema technology to put you on TV to play basketball against one of the NBA's top players. You can also try Virtual Hang Gliding, which sends you soaring like a bird through the Grand Canyon, and WonderCoaster, which challenges your roller coaster-designing skills and then your nerve to ride your creation in a simulator. WonderWorks also runs a laser-tag venue and a twice-nightly magic show, both of which cost extra. *See p45.*

🅢 *Pointe Orlando, 9067 International Dr • Map T4 • 407-351-8800 • Open 9am–midnight daily • Adm*

Titanic – The Experience

This exhibit's 200 artifacts include a real life jacket and an old deck chair, which were both recovered from the wreckage of the fateful liner, as well as the Titanic's second-class passenger list. The attraction also has full-scale re-creations of some of the ship's rooms, including its grand

Titanic – The Experience

staircase, as well as memorabilia from three major Titanic movies – including one of the costumes worn by Leonardo DiCaprio. Actors in period garb play out events that occured on the fateful journey, telling the story of the White Star Line's supposedly unsinkable ship. Most of the artifacts came out of private collections from both the United Kingdom and the USA. *See p44.*

🅢 *The Mercado, 8445 International Dr • Map T3 • 407-248-1166 • Open 10am–10pm daily • Adm*

I-Ride Trolley

One of the best things about I-Drive itself is the tourist-oriented I-Ride Trolley, which offers an easy way to ogle some of the area's oddities and its high-density visual overload. It is also an excellent and extremely cheap way to get around this part of town while avoiding the need to get involved in fighting I-Drive's frustratingly heavy traffic, or walking any distance in the heat. There are 46 stops on the circuit, serving all the local major attractions, shopping malls, hotels, and restaurants. *See p127.*

Around Town – International Drive Area

Left **Ice Bar** Center **Ripleys Believe it or Not! Odditorium** Right **Sports Dominator**

🔟 Eye-Openers on I-Drive

1 Sheraton Studio City Hotel
This distinctive 21-story circular hotel has a Deco-inspired interior design and lighting theme. ⑤ *5905 International Dr • Map T2*

2 Titanic – The Experience
Relive the tragedy, share in the inspirational personal stories of those aboard, and marvel at the splendor of this luxurious liner that has been impressively re-created. *See p99.*

3 Gator Alley Gift Shop
This gift shop is unmissable for anyone who loves Florida's favorite animal, the gator. Every kind of gator-related souvenir is available. ⑤ *7603 International Dr • Map T3 • 407-345-8211*

4 Bargain World
The doorway to this shop is straddled by a large flying saucer. Alighting from a nearby rocketship is a giant green Martian wearing casual clothes and holding a stick. ⑤ *8520 International Dr • Map T2 • 407-351-8876*

5 Sports Dominator
Giant, stern-faced effigies of sports people flank the entrance – one muscle-bound guy in tight pants looks like a reject from the Village People. ⑤ *6464 International Dr • Map T2 • 407-354-2100*

6 Ice Bar
There's always something cool happening at this frozen cocktail bar, from karaoke and swing dance lessons to DJs. Be sure to grab your coat before you visit! ⑤ *8967 International Dr • Map T2*

7 Ripley's Believe It or Not! Odditorium
This place is built to look as if one of Florida's sinkholes opened up and nearly swallowed the building. *See p98.*

8 SkyVenture
Take a close look at this blue and purple building and you might see people floating in front of you – look closer and you will see they are actually flying. *See p45.*

9 WonderWorks
As the marketing story goes, a tornado picked up this four-story building and sent it crashing upside down on top of a 1930s-era brick warehouse. Silly perhaps, but it stops traffic. *See p99.*

10 Air Florida Helicopters
With flights starting at just $20 (kids) and $25 (adults), there's no reason not to enjoy a panoramic birds-eye view over the city. ⑤ *8990 International Dr • Map T4 • 407-354-1400 • 9:30am–8pm daily*

For tips on shopping in Orlando **See p132**

Left **Edwin Watts Golf National Clearance Center** Right **Stores on I-Drive**

TOP 10 I-Drive Stores & Outlet Centers

Nike Factory Store
A gigantic collection of all things adorned with the famous "swoosh," at discount prices. ◈ *Prime Factory Outlet, 5201 W. Oak Ridge Rd • Map U1 • 407-351-9400*

Kenneth Cole
Choose from recent lines of urbane Cole shoes; bags and clothes also vie for attention with about 25 per cent discount. ◈ *Belz Designer Outlet Center, 5247 International Dr • Map U1 • 407-903-1191*

Prime Factory Outlet
With more than 170 stores bursting with bargains, there's something for everyone. ◈ *5401 W. Oakridge Rd • Map U1 • 407-352-9611*

Bass Pro Shops Outdoor World
Overflowing with fishing, golf, camping, and hunting supplies, plus footwear and apparel, this is a vast shrine to the great outdoors. ◈ *5156 International Dr • Map U1 • 407-563-5200*

Coach Factory Store
Leather rules at this spacious store, and deals abound on both current and last season's handbags, jackets, luggage, and more. ◈ *Prime Designer Outlet Center, 5269 International Drive • Map U1 • 407-352-6772*

Edwin Watts Golf National Clearance Center
Like cars, golf clubs also have model years. This store offers last season's hot drivers and putters at deep savings. ◈ *7024 International Dr • Map T3 • 407-352-2535*

Brooks Brothers Outlet
Slim pickings for suits, but there's a great range of casual sportswear for men and women, discounted by at least 40 per cent. ◈ *Orlando Premium Outlets, 8200 Vineland Ave • Map G3 • 407-239-9000*

Off 5th
Like Sak's Fifth Avenue's regular stores, this outlet is heavy on high fashion brand names and has a rapid turnover. ◈ *Prime Designer Outlet Center, 5253 International Dr • Map U1 • 407-354-5757*

Fossil Company Store
The impulse-buy watches at Fossil are cheap, fun, and have a pop-culture aesthetic. ◈ *Prime Designer Outlet Center, 5229 International Dr • Map U1 • 407-352-4107*

Divers Direct Outlet
This deep discount outlet carries everything needed for underwater adventures. The helpful sales team give good advice. ◈ *5403 International Dr • Map U1 • 407-354-3644*

Left **CityJazz** Right **Hard Rock Live**

Bars, Clubs, & Entertainment

Hard Rock Live
One of the best spots in to see live music (national/local rock and R&B acts), with a top-notch sound system. *See p74.* ✪ *City-Walk • Map T1 • 407-351-5483 • Adm*

The Groove
This powerhouse dance club has slamming DJs, as well as several quiet chill-out lounges. *See p77.* ✪ *CityWalk • Map T1 • 407-224-3663 • Over 21 yrs • Adm*

Jimmy Buffet's Margaritaville
A mecca for Parrot Heads or anyone who wants to have a good time in the ultimate tropical setting. Great drinks, food, and live entertainment most evenings. ✪ *Universal CityWalk • Map T1 • 407-224-2155*

Glo Lounge
This upscale lounge has an upbeat ambience with deco flair and plenty of neon. It attracts a lively dinner crowd. ✪ *8967 International Dr • 407-351-0361 • Map T4 • Free*

Lucky Leprechaun
Karaoke every night at this lively and popular Irish-themed bar – great selection of Irish beers. ✪ *7032 International Dr • Map T4 • 407-352-7031*

Latin Quarter
Expect anything Latin – from food to dance lessons – at this energetic venue. A 13-piece Latin band is on most nights. ✪ *CityWalk • Map T1 • 407-224-2800 • Adm after 10pm Thu–Sat*

Adobe Gilas
Crowds of 20-somethings swarm this restaurant/bar (with 65 varieties of tequila) and dance the night away. *See p75.* ✪ *Pointe Orlando, 9101 International Dr • Map T4 • 407-903-1477 • Free • DA*

Bob Marley – A Tribute To Freedom
Live outdoor reggae music is the big draw here, and the bands are often excellent. ✪ *CityWalk • Map T1 • 407-224-2690 • Over 21 yrs only after 10pm • Occasional evening adm*

Cricketers Arms Pub
A little piece of England, with European soccer on the TVs, darts, and nearly 20 ales, lagers, bitters, and stouts on tap. ✪ *Mercado, 8445 International Dr • Map T3 • 407-354-0686 • Free*

CityJazz
This beautiful and acoustically vibrant room emulates the big, urbane jazz supper clubs of the past. ✪ *CityWalk • Map T1 • 407-224-2189 • Occasional adm*

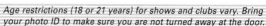

Age restrictions (18 or 21 years) for shows and clubs vary. Bring your photo ID to make sure you are not turned away at the door.

Price Categories

For a three-course meal for one, a glass of house wine and all unavoidable extra charges including tax.	**$** under $20
	$$ $20–$30
	$$$ $30–$45
	$$$$ $45–$60
	$$$$$ over $60

Ran-Getsu of Tokyo

🔟 Places to Eat

Café Tu Tu Tango
Local artists' work adorns the walls of this vaguely Latin-style eatery. Dishes include black bean soup, shrimp fritters, and quesadillas. ➅ *8625 International Dr • Map T3 • 407-248-2222 • $$*

Ran-Getsu of Tokyo
High-class Japanese tourists endorse Ran-Getsu's authentic dishes, ranging from sushi to teriyaki. *See p69.* ➅ *8400 International Dr • Map T4 • 407-345-0044 • $$$$*

Roy's
On the menu here are Hawaiian fusion dishes such as sesame-oil-seared mahi-mahi with red Thai curry sauce. ➅ *7760 W. Sand Lake Rd • S3 • 407-352-4844 • $$$$*

The Butcher Shop
Enjoy big juicy steaks in this gorgeous dining room. You can even grill your own steak if you wish. ➅ *8445 International Dr • Map T3 • 407-363-9727 • No kids' menu • $$$$$*

Seasons 52
The seasonally inspired menu includes grilled vegetables, crab-stuffed mushrooms, and rosemary and parmesan cheese flatbreads. All dishes have a low calorie content. ➅ *7700 W. Sandlake Road • 407-354-5212 • No kids' menu • $$$*

Cuba Libre
Located in a Cuban hacienda courtyard, Cuba Libre serves Cuban cuisine and has choreographed floor shows on Saturday nights. ➅ *Pointe Orlando, 9101 International Dr • Map T4 • 407-226-1600 • $$$$*

NBA City
This is the place where you can cheer for your favorite team on TV while you eat. Enjoy the NBA memorabilia on the walls during the ad breaks. ➅ *Universal CityWalk • Map T1 • 407-363-5919 • $$*

Bahama Breeze
Trust the Caribbean menu and spirits to create some fun, but expect to wait up to two hours for a table. ➅ *8849 International Dr • Map T4 • 407-248-2499 • No reservations • $$$*

Chili's Grill & Bar
One of the better chains offering Tex-Mex food including fajitas, sandwiches, and grills, with low-fat options. ➅ *7021 International Dr • T2 • 407-352-7618 • $$$*

The Palm
Think high-end steaks, often belly-busters (up to a 36-oz [1.2-kg] strip for two) but don't overlook the lobster option. ➅ *Hard Rock Hotel, 5800 Universal Blvd • Map T1 • 407-503-7256 • $$$$$*

Unless stated, all restaurants advise reservations, are non-smoking, take credit cards, and have DA, kids' menus, A/C, and vegetarian dishes.

Left **Osceola County Historical Museum & Pioneer Center** Right **Gatorland**

Kissimmee

WHAT USED TO BE A COW TOWN *has in the past few decades evolved into an inexpensive hotel enclave for Disney World tourists. But there's more to Kissimmee than cheap places to sleep. Though U.S. 192 (also called the Irlo Bronson Memorial Highway) is dense with strip malls and hotels – and looks like a grim vision of tourist hell – downtown Kissimmee (centered on Broadway and Emmet streets) was built in the early 1890s and boasts attractive low-slung buildings, which house several antique and gift shops. The land surrounding U.S. 192 is relatively undeveloped, providing Kissimmee visitors with easy access to Florida's rich, natural beauty. A terrific variety of outdoor pursuits is available to the visitor who is willing to spend time away from the theme parks.*

Downtown Kissimmee

TOP 10 Sights & Attractions

1. Gatorland
2. Celebration
3. World of Orchids
4. Osceola County Historical Museum & Pioneer Center
5. Green Meadows Petting Farm
6. Lakefront Park
7. Old Town
8. Reptile World Serpentarium
9. Forever Florida – Florida Eco-Safaris
10. Silver Spurs Rodeo

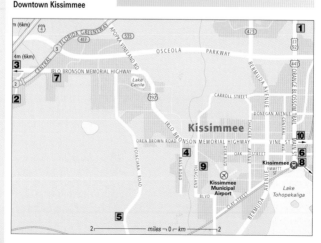

World of Orchids

Gatorland

Gatorland, Orlando's original theme park, opened more than 50 years ago as a swampy road-side stand, and is now home to well over 1,000 alligators, crocodiles, and snakes. Its appeal? A chance to gaze, just steps away from these mysterious creatures, who remain curiously similar to their prehistoric relatives. Visitors can stroll along a boardwalk over lakes full of cranky gators and buy hot dogs to throw into their mouths. A bizarre and unique attraction. *See p44.* ◊ *14501 S. Orange Blossom Trail • Map G4 • 800-393-5297 • Open 9am–sunset daily • Adm*

Celebration

When Walt Disney conceived of Epcot *(see pp12–15)*, he imagined it as a residential community happily engaged in road-testing futuristic technologies. After his death, that dream went out the window only to resurface years later here. However, instead of looking to the future, Celebration salutes the past in a cliché of small town USA (think *The Truman Show*). The houses are pretty, the downtown has some good restaurants and a cinema, and everything is upscale. This is not an attraction, but it is quite a sight. ◊ *Located E. of I-4 at Exit 25. Turn right at Celebration Ave and follow the signs • Map G2*

World of Orchids

This unusual and serene spot was founded in 1983 by a couple who moved north when their Miami orchid nursery was destroyed by Hurricane Andrew. There are more than 1,000 orchids on display in the conservatory and outside on the nature walk, both of which are densely and beautifully landscaped. *See p45.* ◊ *2501 Old Lake Wilson Rd • Map H1 • 407-396-1887 • Open 9:30am–4:30pm Mon–Sat • Free • www.aworldoforchids.com*

Osceola County Historical Museum & Pioneer Center

This homespun outdoor museum gives a glimpse of Kissimmee life before Disney. The focal point is a pair of late 1800s "Cracker-style" cypress wood buildings, complete with "possum trot" breezeway – an early form of air-conditioning. One showcases a simple home, while the other is reconfigured as a general store, selling local history books, crafts, and guides for the nature preserve located across the street. ◊ *750 N. Bass Rd • Map H3 • 407-396-8644 • Open Thu–Sat 10am–4pm, 1pm–4pm Sun • Adm*

Green Meadows Petting Farm

This educational spot is perfect for anyone who might enjoy milking a cow, riding a pony, or learning about over 300 friendly farm animals. A two-hour guided tour is included and picnic facilities are available. ◊ *1368 S. Poinciana Blvd • Map H3 • 407-846-0770 • Open 9:30am–4pm daily • Adm*

Green Meadows Petting Farm

6 Lakefront Park

This park offers a range of amenities, such as pavilions, picnic areas, and playgrounds, and hosts many community events and concerts. There are several miles of pathways for walkers, joggers, skaters, and bicycles, including a sidewalk by Lake Tohopekaliga that is

Lakefront Park

popular with birdwatchers. It also has a superb white sand beach, a fishing pier, and impressive marina. The park has easy access to Kissimmee's historic district, and is close to Chisholm Park and Peghorn Nature Park. *See p48.*
⌖ *1104 Lakefront Blvd, St. Cloud • Map H6*

7 Old Town

Essentially, this is a tourist-oriented shopping mall filled with around 75 stores covering the usual array of gifts, novelty items, and souvenirs – kitsch or otherwise. What sets Old Town apart from other gift-shop strips are the numerous entertainment options: a cheerful 18-ride amusement park, Laser Tag, a Haunted

House, carousel, live music performances, and a vintage car show every Friday and Saturday night. It's very much about family fun, and there's no charge for admission, although the carnival rides are priced separately. On a warm Florida night, the feeling is one of strolling the bustling midway of a state fair. ⌖ *5770 W. Irlo Bronson Hwy • Map G2 • Open 10am–11pm daily • Free*

8 Reptile World Serpentarium

This is a unique and educational attraction providing all the right ingredients to make your skin crawl. Visitors can watch a snake handler extracting poisonous venom from cobras, rattlesnakes, and other deadly serpents. The indoor exhibits house more than 60 species of reptiles, and it's the largest of its kind in central Florida. *See p45.* ⌖ *5705 E. Irlo Bronson Memorial Hwy (3.5 miles east of St. Cloud) • Map H6 • Open 9am–5:30pm Tue–Sun • Adm*

9 Forever Florida – Florida Eco-Safaris

Go back in time to Old Florida on this working cattle ranch and nature preserve. The Forever Florida experience is based on the heritage of the Florida Cracker Cowboy. Take a tour on horseback or ride aboard an elevated cracker coach, then in the evening enjoy a

Forever Florida – Florida Eco-Safaris

Vintage cars, Old Town

meal at the Cypress Restaurant.
⊛ 4755 N. Kenansville Road, St. Cloud •
407-957-9794 • Eco-Safaris on Safari
Coaches at 10am and 1pm daily •
www.floridaeco-safaris.com

Silver Spurs Rodeo
The largest rodeo held east
of the Mississippi, attracts all the
top professional cowboys and is
held several times a year. The
Silver Spurs Rodeo dates back to
1944 and was from 1950 held in
a specially constructed open-air
arena, until that was replaced by
the state-of-the-art, climate-
controlled Silver Spurs Arena in
2002. The arena is also used for
many other events, such as
concerts and sports, but will
always be chiefly associated with
the excitement of bronc riding,
steer wrestling, and bull riding.
⊛ Osceola Heritage Park, 1875 Silver
Spur Lane • Map H5 • 407-67-RODEO •
www.silverspursrodeo.com

Silver Spurs Rodeo

A Day in Kissimmee

Morning

There are countless breakfast buffets in the area, all
offering mounds of food,
from fresh fruit to omelets.
Find the one closest to you
and start the day there. As
mornings tend to be cooler
and a bit less insect-ridden
than afternoons, follow your
meal with a self-guided tour
of swamp life at **Airboat
Rentals You Drive** (see
p110). Head as far away as
possible from the the road,
cut the engine, and enjoy
the silence. Most of Florida
used to be like this. For
lunch, head to Kissimmee's
historic Downtown and pop
in to Azteca's (809 N. Main
St), a tiny and original Tex-
Mex restaurant. Be careful
ordering anything "very
hot"; the cook takes this as
a personal challenge and
will likely spice the dish
so your head explodes.

Afternoon

From Downtown, it's a
short drive north to **Gatorland**. The massive gators
prowling the front lakes are
the big attraction. But smart
guests will take the Swamp
Walk, check out the croco-
dile pens, and survey the
alligator breeding marsh
from the observation tower.
There are four live animal
shows but if time is tight,
Gator Jump-A-Roo and Gator
Wrestling are the essentials.

Evening

For dinner, the slightly camp
Pacino's Italian Ristorante
(see p111) is popular for its
home-style Italian favorites
and delicious pizza. After-
wards, take another short
drive to **Old Town** where
kids can play on the rides
while adults watch from a
bench enjoying an ice cream.

Left **Airboat ride, Boggy Creek** Center **Fishing, Kissimmee** Right **Warbird Adventures**

Leisure Pursuits & Activities

1 East Lake Fish Camp
This lakeside facility provides everything from fishing poles to boats, bait, and bunks. Large mouth bass and sometimes game fish hit the lines. ✆ 3705 Big Bass Rd • Off map • 407-348-2040 • Adm • No DA

2 Jetski Sports
Here's the place to race around on one- to three-seat motorcycles for the water. ✆ 4960 W. Irlo Bronson Memorial Hwy • Map G3 • 407-390-0091 • Adm • No DA

3 Warbird Adventures
Have a flight in a vintage North American T-6 Texan or a Bell 47 helicopter. You'll even get the chance to take the controls and have the whole experience video-taped. ✆ 233 N. Hoagland Blvd • Map H3 • 407-870-7366

4 Airboat Rentals You Drive
After instruction, take off in a small airboat to commune with nature deep in a cypress swamp. ✆ 4266 W. Hwy 192 • Map H3 • 407-847-3672 • Adm • No DA

5 Osceola Center For The Arts
Here, culture mavens will find anything from theater to music events, and exhibitions. ✆ 2411 E. Irlo Bronson Memorial Hwy • Map H5 • 407-846-6257 • Adm

6 Boggy Creek Airboat Rides
These 18-passenger flat-bottomed skiffs powered by giant fans make regular daylight wildlife tours and special one-hour night tours. ✆ 3702 Big Bass Rd • Off map • 407-344-9550 • Adm

7 The Ice Factory
Get out of the Florida sun and do a few laps on this ice rink, which also has a kids' play area. ✆ 2221 Partin Settlement Rd • Map H5 • 407-933-4259 • Adm • No DA

8 Falcon's Fire Golf Club
This immaculately groomed public golf course is said to be one of the best in Florida. ✆ 3200 Seralago Blvd • Map G3 • 407-239-5445 • Adm • No DA • www.falconsfire.com

9 Central Florida Guide Service
This professional guide service takes clients fishing in some of the best big bass waters in Florida. ✆ 1326 Sweetwood Blvd • Map H4 • 407-908-4600 • Adm • www.floridabassfishing.com

10 Horse World Riding Stables
Enjoy horse riding on 750 acres (300 ha) of peaceful sandy trails. There are pony and hay rides, as well as friendly farm animals. ✆ 3705 S. Poinciana Blvd • Off map • 407-847-4343 • Adm

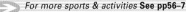

Price Categories

For a three-course meal for one with a glass of house wine, and all unavoidable extra charges including tax.

$	under $20
$$	$20–$30
$$$	$30–$45
$$$$	$45–$60
$$$$$	over $60

Tarantino's Italian Restaurant

🔟 Places to Eat

Charley's Steak House
Charley's uses an Indian cooking method, yielding steaks that are charred outside, juicy inside. ◈ *2901 Parkway Blvd • Map G2 • 407-239-1270 • Closed lunch • $$$$*

Azteca's Mexican
Authentic Mexican and Tex-Mex is served in an extravagantly decorated room. ◈ *809 N. Main St • Map H4 • 407-933-8155 • $$ • No DA*

Tarantino's Italian Restaurant
This delightful Italian venue wins praise for charming ambience and well-prepared Italian classics. ◈ *10 W. Monument • Map H3 • 407-870-2622 • Closed lunch • $$$*

Magic Mining Steaks and Seafood Company
Ribs, steaks, chicken – anything that can fit on a grill. Kids will love the gold mine decor and the electric train running through the restaurant. ◈ *7736 W. Hwy 192 • Map G1 • 407-396-1950 • Open daily • $$*

Pacino's Italian Ristorante
Sicilian specialties here include hand-cut steaks, veal chops, and great pizza and pasta. ◈ *5795 W. Irlo Bronson Memorial Hwy • Map G2 • 407-396-8022 • $$$$*

Puerto Rico Café
It's a bit of a dive, but don't let that put you off trying the delicious *mojo*-enhanced steaks and seafood. ◈ *507 W. Vine St • Map H4 • 407-847-6399 • Open daily • $$$ • No DA*

Asia Bagus
The menu at this Indonesian restaurant includes Singapore rice noodles and a comprehensive selection of *rijsttafel* dishes. ◈ *2923 Vineland Rd • Map G3 • 407-397-2205 • Closed Sun in Sep • $$$*

Black Angus Restaurant
Melt-in-your-mouth steaks are the focus of this award-winning, family eatery, but ribs and fried chicken are also popular. There's a great breakfast buffet, too. ◈ *7516 W. Irlo Bronson Memorial Hwy • Map G1 • 407-390-4548 • $$$$*

Logan's Roadhouse
With its neon signs and country jukebox, the vibe here is 1940s, honky-tonk, roadside grill. Try the mesquite-grilled steaks or honey sweet rolls. ◈ *5925 W. Irlo Bronson Memorial Hwy • Map G2 • 407-390-0500 • $$$*

Ocean 11
The nautical decor is a bit kitsch, but nothing's wrong with the fish and seafood dished up here. Order it in any number of ways (including blackened). There are plenty of non-fish options, too. ◈ *2901 Parkway Blvd • Map G2 • 407-396-7736 • Closed lunch • $$$$*

Unless stated, all restaurants advise reservations, are non-smoking, take credit cards, have DA, kids' menus, A/C, and vegetarian dishes.

Left **Downtown Skyline** Right **Orange County Regional History Center**

Downtown Orlando

MOST FOLKS ASSUME ORLANDO IS *just about Walt Disney and amusement parks, with the odd cowboy and conservative Christian thrown in for good measure. But that's not the case. Long a state capital for the banking and citrus industries, Orlando's Downtown also contains several of the city's leading museums, as well as its best-known park, a lovely green oasis that surrounds Lake Eola, which boasts dramatic skyline vistas. By day Downtown is a relaxed southern enclave, but by night it transforms into a throbbing club scene – despite the decline of the famous entertainment, dining, and shopping zone, Church Street Station. Orange Avenue is the main street and most evenings, herds of party people, both gay and straight, migrate from club to club in search of cheap drinks and hot DJs – and there are plenty of both.*

Orlando Science Center

🔟 Sights

1. Orlando Science Center
2. Orlando Museum of Art
3. Orange County Regional History Center
4. Harry P. Leu Gardens
5. Mennello Museum of American Folk Art
6. The Vietnamese District
7. Lake Eola Park
8. Orlando Hauntings Ghost Tours
9. Church Street
10. Colonial Lanes

Orlando Science Center

The workings of the natural world, from the infinitesimal to the overwhelming, are on display here. Big interactive fun awaits at the Body Zone, where a huge mouth introduces an exhibit about the digestive system. The vast Cinedome shows movies about topics such as Egyptian treasures and ocean life, and on weekend evenings, stargazers can pick out the planets through a telescope. ⊗ 777 E. Princeton St • Map M3 • 407-514-2000 • Open 10am–6pm Sun–Tue, 10am–9pm Wed & Thu, 10am–11pm Fri & Sat • Adm • www.osc.org

Orlando Museum of Art (OMA)

The focus of exhibitions in this big, bright museum is American art from the 19th century onward, art from the ancient Americas and Africa, and blockbuster traveling shows. On the first Thursday evening of every month, you can enjoy music, food, and the work of local artists for an inventively themed get-together. ⊗ 2416 N. Mills Ave • Map M3 • 407-896-4231 • 10am–4pm Tue–Fri, noon–4pm Sat–Sun • Adm • www.omart.org

Orange County Regional History Center

From the informative to the kitsch, the History Center highlights the formative periods and industries of Central Florida. Dioramas show scenes of early Native Americans, and a re-created Florida Cracker house can be inspected. There's also a display called The Day We Changed, which chronicles the impact of the arrival of the Disney theme parks. Some exhibits fall a little flat, but many elements, such as the stuffed alligators and pink flamingos, betray a sense of fun. ⊗ 65 E. Central Blvd • Map P3 • 407-836-8500 • 10am–5pm Mon–Sat, noon–5pm Sun • Adm • www.thehistorycenter.org

Harry P. Leu Gardens

Well-tended pathways weave through this elegant 50-acre (20-ha) park. Earthy scents waft from an herb garden, while another contains plants that attract butterflies. Depending on the season, visitors might catch roses in bloom (in Florida's largest rose garden) or the grace of camellias. Guides conduct tours of the early 20th-century Leu House. ⊗ 1920 N. Forest Ave • Map M4 • 407-246-2620 • Open 9am–5pm daily • Adm • www.leugardens.org

Fountain, Lake Eola Park

Mennello Museum of American Folk Art

Half of the Mennello is devoted to the work of Florida folk artist Earl Cunningham (1893–1977), who created vibrant, whimsical pastoral paintings glowing with orange skies and yellow rivers. The other half houses traveling exhibits of folk art. The lakeside grounds contain wonderfully quirky sculptures scattered here and there. ⊗ 900 E. Princeton St • Map M3 • 407-246-4278 • 10:30am–4:30pm Tue–Sat, noon–4:30pm Sun • Adm • www.mennellomuseum.com

Mennello Museum of American Folk Art

The Vietnamese District

This area, also known as the ViMi district (for the crossroads at Virginia and Mills avenues), is a less obvious ethnic enclave than, say, New York's Chinatown. Nevertheless, it is still clustered with Vietnamese restaurants and shops, as well as delights from other Asian countries. The thickest concentration is south of Virginia, at Colonial Drive. ◎ *Mills Ave bet Virginia Ave & Colonial Dr • Map N3*

Lake Eola Park

A pedestrian-only path encircles Lake Eola, offering a pleasing view of Downtown's skyline. Those willing to exert their leg muscles can rent swan-shaped paddle boats (*see p47*). Real swans drift along in the lake's shallow water and will venture onto dry land if offered a handful of the food that can be bought for small change. Plays and concerts are performed at the Walt Disney Amphitheater, a bandshell with surprisingly decent acoustics. Disney's presence is more ostentatiously displayed with the rather incongruous Millennium clock located on the lake's southern side. ◎ *Map P3*

Signs, Vietnamese Disctrict

Orlando Hauntings Ghost Tours

A guide in 19th-century costume holds a lantern and tries his best to spook his willing participants, while leading this 90-minute walking tour. Groups of up to 25 people hear tales of murder, morbidity, and ghost sightings, and as an added bonus, the guide recounts wonderful anecdotes and information about the architecture and history of Downtown's most interesting buildings. ◎ *Depart from Guinevere's coffee house, at Pine St & Magnolia Ave • Map P3 • 407-992-1200 • 8pm every Fri and Sat • Adm*

Church Street

The stretch of Church Street that lies between Orange Avenue and I-4 is thick with enough specialty shops, restaurants, and bars to keep visitors engaged for hours. The anchor is Church Street Station, although the closure of several of its restaurants and shows has lessened the appeal of the complex. Despite this slowdown, the bar strip on the eastern side of Church Street near Orange Avenue remains very popular, especially with its three-level complex that has different bars on each floor. On weekend evenings, the street is blocked to traffic, which makes it easy to zigzag between watering holes such as the Ybor Martini Bar and Mulvaney's, although hipper bars are found around the corner on Orange Avenue (*see p116*). ◎ *Church St bet. Orange Ave & I-4 • Map P3*

Lake Eola Fountain, Lake Eola Park

Church Street

Colonial Lanes

For more than 50 years, the venerable Colonial Lanes has offered patrons the sociable and quintessential blue-collar pastime of bowling. This 32-lane facility is a friendly and noisy place to knock over a few pins, so rent some shoes, pick out a ball, and let the computer keep score – but bear in mind that league bowling takes over the place between 6pm and 9pm every night, so

Bowling balls, Colonial Lanes

avoid those times, unless you're happy to watch. After the game, the place to go is the Colonial Lanes Bar & Restaurant, parts of which resemble a giant sunken living room (with bartenders standing on a lower floor than customers). Drinks are cheap, and the concept of rounding off prices never caught on here, so don't be surprised if your tab is a quirky $4.38. ◈ *400 N. Primrose Dr • Map P4 • 407-894-0361 • 9am–midnight daily • Free, but pay to play*

A Day Downtown

Morning

Begin with a big healthy breakfast at JP's Everyday Gourmet (63 E. Pine St) before visiting the **Orange County Regional History Center**, a homespun place that reveals the pre-Disney history of the region. For lunch, wander over to **Café Annie** *(see p117)*. This authentic café has Greek and Lebanese food, including mixed platters. This kind of food usually has lots of vegetarian options.

Afternoon

After lunch, jump in the car or grab a cab to Loch Haven Park, where the **Orlando Museum of Art**, the **Orlando Science Center,** and the **Mennello Museum of American Folk Art** *(for all see p113)* reside within easy walking distance of each other. The Science Center, with its four floors of interactive fun, is the best bet for kids. Art lovers can easily hit the Mennello and the OMA in the same afternoon but if time is short, the OMA deserves priority. Make a dinner stop in the Vietnamese district where Vinh's Restaurant (1231 E. Colonial Dr) serves up a top-notch bowl of comforting *pho*, a traditional, and delicious noodle soup.

Evening

The downtown club scene starts late, so kick off with an early cocktail at **The Bösendorfer Lounge** *(see p116)*. Fans of live music should head to **The Social** *(see p116)*, where shows start around 10pm. Diehard clubbers should try **The Club at Firestone** *(see p76)*, where the DJs play well into the early hours.

Left **The Social** Right **Tabu**

Nightspots

The Social
Orlando's best club for live music, bar none. The stage hosts an incredible variety of performers, from jazz to electronica. *See p74.* 🔊 *54 N. Orange Ave • Map P3 • 407-246-1419*

Tabu
This cavernous former theater is a dark and trendy magnet, largely for 20-somethings on the prowl. The music favors house and breakbeat. 🔊 *46 N. Orange Ave • Map P3 • 407-648-8363 • Closed Mon*

Cowboys Orlando
This gigantic country music hot spot has four huge bars and nightly dance contests. 🔊 *1108 S. Orange Blossom Trail • Map P2 • 407-422-7115 • Closed Sun–Wed*

The Bösendorfer Lounge
With upscale elegance, this lounge is perfect for sipping cocktails in stylish surroundings. Lounge singers and pianists play around the $250,000 Bösendorfer piano (Tue–Sat). *See p74.* 🔊 *Westin Grand Bohemian Hotel, 325 S. Orange Ave • Map P3 • 866-663-0024*

Dragon Room
This fun watering hole with a great DJ is usually packed. Women get in free until midnight on Wednesdays. 🔊 *25 W. Church St • Map P2 • Open 9pm till late Wed–Sat • 407-843-8600 • Adm*

Sky 60
South Beach-style hip bar with a DJ every night. Great rooftop terrace with mood lighting. 🔊 *64 N. Orange Ave • Map P3 • 407-246-1599*

Church Street
A two-block strip of bars, restaurants, and clubs that draws party people wanting to steer clear of the trendiness of other downtown clubs. 🔊 *Church St, bet Orange Ave & I-4 • Map P3*

The Club at Firestone
This club offers lively techno, rave, and house dance beats. The best time to go is on the weekends, especially Saturday nights when there is a big crowd and occasional live acts. 🔊 *578 N. Orange Ave • Map N3 • 407-872-0066*

Eye Spy
Espionage is the theme at this bar, with rooms behind bookcases and spy gadgets everywhere. Attracts a lively singles crowd. 🔊 *64 N. Orange Ave • Map P3 • 407-246-1599*

Independent Bar
This club is multi-leveled with state-of-the-art sound and light systems, three bars, and two dance floors with differing styles of music. 🔊 *70 N. Orange Ave • Map P3 • 407-839-0457 • www.independentbar.net*

Unless indicated Downtown's nightspots are open seven nights a week.

Price Categories

For a three-course meal for one with a glass of house wine, and all unavoidable extra charges including tax.

$	under $20
$$	$20–$30
$$$	$30–$45
$$$$	$45–$60
$$$$$	over $60

The Black Olive

🔟 Restaurants & Cafés

1 K Restaurant and Wine Bar
Downtown's best dining experience mixes bistro warmth with an adventurous menu of Asian, French, and Italian influences. ◈ 2401 Edgewater Dr • Map M2 • 407-872-2332 • Closed Sun, Mon • $$$$

2 The Boheme
This outstanding restaurant, with its sensual paintings and dark woods, serves game, steaks, and seafood to an upscale clientele. See p69. ◈ 325 S. Orange Ave • Map P3 • 407-581-4700 • $$$$$

3 Napasorn Thai Restaurant
This family-owned restaurant serves traditional Thai dishes and interesting pan-Asian variations. ◈ 56 E. Pine St • Map P2 • 407-245-8088 • Closed lunch Sat & Sun • $$$

4 Graffiti Junction American Burger Bar
The graffiti-covered exterior belies a great, high-energy burger joint within. Order the huge "Lone Star" for a messy delight. There is karaoke on Sunday afternoons. ◈ 900 E. Washington St • Map P2 • 407-426-9502 • $$

5 Café Annie
Head here for authentic Greek and Lebanese food, especially Zorba's platter, the chicken and beef kebabs, couscous and falafel. ◈ 131 N. Orange Ave • Map P3 • 407-420-4041 • Closed Sun • $$$

6 Dexter's of Thornton Park
A favorite after-work hangout, Dexter's offers exotic sandwiches, hearty salads, and entrées such as seared tuna and steak. ◈ 808 E. Washington St • Map P3 • 407-648-2777 • $$$

7 Ceviche Tapas Bar & Restaurant
Huge, noisy, and loads of fun, this restaurant offers an enormous menu, a tapas bar, and a large lounge with live flamenco music. ◈ 125 W. Church St • Map P2 • 321-281-8140 • Closed lunch, Sun • $$$

8 Little Saigon
This venue stands out in the city's thriving Vietnamese area for its huge bowls of *pho*, fragrant soup brimming with meat, seafood, noodles, and spices. ◈ 1106 E. Colonial Dr • Map N3 • 407-423-8539 • $$

9 White Wolf Café
This café serves great salads and Middle-Eastern-inspired fare in a former antiques store. It also sells most of its vintage furnishings. ◈ 1829 N. Orange Ave • Map N3 • 407-895-5590 • $$$

10 The Black Olive
A Mediterranean menu of ravioli, pan-seared lamb chops, and daily fresh fish is coupled with sterling service at this stylish venue. ◈ 22 E. Pine St • Map P2 • 407-849-1689 • Closed Sat lunch, Sun • $$$$

Unless stated, all restaurants advise reservations, are non-smoking, take credit cards, have DA, kids' menus, A/C, and vegetarian dishes.

Left **Winter Park street scene** Right **Cornell Fine Arts Museum**

Winter Park, Maitland, & Eatonville

TRUE TO ITS NAME, Winter Park was chartered in 1887 as a winter resort for wealthy – and cold – Northerners. It evolved into a suburb of metropolitan Orlando, but still retains the charm and character of a wealthy, small town, with excellent shops, bars, and restaurants, and a sprinkling of interesting museums. The areas of Maitland and Eatonville, to the north and east, are more residential, but also have some worthwhile attractions, which make a pleasant change from south Orlando's mass-market theme parks.

Winter Park Scenic Boat Tour

🔟 Sights & Attractions

1. Park Avenue
2. Charles Hosmer Morse Museum of American Art
3. Cornell Fine Arts Museum
4. Winter Park Scenic Boat Tour
5. Albin Polasek Museum & Sculpture Gardens
6. Waterhouse Residence & Carpentry Museum
7. Birds of Prey Center
8. Zora Neale Hurston National Museum of Fine Arts
9. Winter Park Farmers' Market
10. Enzian Theater

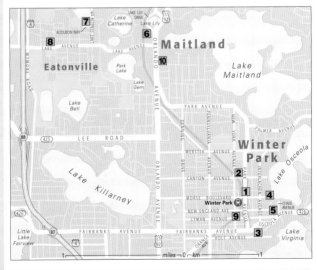

Around Town – Winter Park, Maitland, & Eatonville

Park Avenue

The stretch of Park Avenue between Fairbanks and Swoope avenues is a thriving and delectable slice of urban living. This is the kind of manageable, old-style downtown, which is usually erased in the rush to suburbanize the Sunshine State. There's bucolic Central Park; buildings are rarely over three stories and contain fashionable shops or eateries at ground level; and all around, the sidewalks are full of people enjoying the day. ® Map L4

Park Avenue

range of European and American art – from the Renaissance to the 20th century – is impeccably presented and of an unusually high quality for a small college art museum. ® 100 Holt Ave • Map L4 • 407-646-2526 • Open 10am–5pm Tue–Sat, 1–5pm Sun • Free

Charles Hosmer Morse Museum of American Art

The imposing, windowless walls of this museum rather ironically contain an outstanding collection of beautiful glass windows and objects by the American artist, Louis Comfort Tiffany. Other highlights include American ceramics and representative collections of late-19th- and early-20th-century paintings, graphics, and decorative arts. ® 445 N. Park Ave • Map L4 • 407-645-5311 • Open 9:30am–4pm Tue–Sat (to 8pm Fri Sep–May), 1–4pm Sun • Adm • www.morsemuseum.org

Cornell Fine Arts Museum

The art collection at this museum, located on the scenic Rollins College Campus, is one of the oldest in the state. The

Winter Park Scenic Boat Tour

The wealthiest sections of Winter Park were built by a series of lakes and along small, winding canals. This boat tour has been running since 1938, and is part nature trip and part local history lesson. It cruises lazily past Winter Park landmarks and lakeside mansions encountering wildlife, while the skipper tells stories about the area's legendary society crowd. *See p45.* ® Morse Blvd at Lake Osceola • Map L4 • 407-644-4056 • Tours depart on the hour 10am–4pm daily • Adm

Albin Polasek Museum & Sculpture Gardens

Albin Polasek Museum & Sculpture Gardens

Sculptor Albin Polasek moved here to retire, but in fact he kept producing his figurative works until his death in 1965. Now listed on the National Register of Historic Places, the museum and its sculpture gardens contain works spanning Polasek's entire career. ® 633 Osceola Ave • Map L4 • 407-647-6294 • Open 10am–4pm Tue–Sat, 1–4pm Sun • Adm • www.polasek.org

Charles Hosmer Morse Museum of American Art

Waterhouse Residence & Carpentry Museum

6 Historic Waterhouse Residence & Carpentry Museum

William H. Waterhouse was a carpenter who came to Central Florida in the early 1880s and built this lovely home overlooking Lake Lily. Pristinely restored and maintained by the Maitland Historical Society, the home, Waterhouse's carpentry shop, and the property's remarkable collection of hand-crafted furniture offer a glimpse into the DIY days of Maitland's past. Woodworking buffs will be wowed by Waterhouse's extensive use of heart of pine, a wood rarely seen today. Tours lasting about 40 minutes are offered. The Waterhouse facilities nicely complement the Maitland Historical Museum and the Telephone Museum *(see p61)*, both located just a few blocks away and also run by the Maitland Historical Society. ✪ 820 Lake Lilly Dr
• Map K3 • 407-644-2451 • Open Thu–Sun noon–4pm • Adm
• www.maitlandhistory.org

7 Audubon National Center for Birds of Prey

Think of this place as a halfway house for some of the most impressive examples of Florida's birdlife. It was created by the Florida Audubon Society to rescue, rehabilitate, and release wounded raptors (birds of prey). Those that wouldn't survive being released into the wild are kept here, living a pampered existence in a lovely lakeside location, while helping to educate visitors about wildlife issues and conservation. Guests aren't allowed to observe the rehabilitation process, but permanent residents on view usually include vultures, bald eagles, screech owls, hawks, ospreys, and more.
✪ 1101 Audubon Way • Map K3 • 407 644-0190 • Open 10am–4pm Tue–Sun
• Adm • www.audubonofflorida.org

Birds of Prey Center

8 Zora Neale Hurston National Museum of Fine Arts

Zora Neale Hurston earned fame as one of the brightest stars of Harlem's literary heyday in the 1920 and 1930s. Many of her most famous writings (including the 1937 novel, *Their Eyes Were Watching God*) reflected life in her hometown of Eatonville, the first incorporated African-American municipality in the USA. The front porches and stores of Eatonville, where Zora's characters lived and spun their tales, have long since disappeared, but she is not forgotten. This museum keeps the writer's memory alive, with maps for a self-guided walking tour to the remaining literary landmarks of her neighborhood. The museum also exhibits work by contemporary African-American artists.
✪ 227 E. Kennedy Blvd
• Map K3 • 407-647-3307
• Open 9am–4pm Mon–Fri
• Free • www. zoranealehurston.com

Winter Park Farmers' Market

Some farmers' markets are serious business, packed with old trucks and farmers selling mountains of vegetables just pulled from the earth. The Winter Park Farmers' Market is altogether a different affair. More of a social gathering on the village green, Winter Park's yuppies come here to mingle, buy potted flowers, preserves, and herbs, and indulge in fresh croissants, muffins, and breads. Yes, the required vegetables are here, too, but this is more of a coffee and brunch gathering. ◈ 721 W. England Ave • Map L4 • 407-599-3358 • Open 7am–1pm Sat • Free

Exhibit, Zora Neale Hurston National Museum of Fine Arts

Enzian Theater

The art of film tastes different at the Enzian. This not-for-profit 250-seat theater doesn't just show American independent and foreign films, but also offers a full menu with beer, wine, and table service. Relax with dinner or snacks and enjoy films with all the comforts of your own living room (if that living room has a 33-ft (10-m) wide screen). The Enzian also produces the 10-day Florida Film Festival (see p65) and smaller niche festivals throughout the year. ◈ 1300 S. Orlando Ave • Map K3 • 407-629-1088 • Open evenings daily & weekend afternoons • Adm • www.enzian.org

A Day in Winter Park

Morning

🕘 Begin with a hearty breakfast at the **Briarpatch Restaurant** (see p123). You'll probably have to wait a bit, especially on weekends, so grab a newspaper. Then take time to wander the north end of **Park Avenue** (see p119), where a multitude of charming one-off boutiques cater to upscale shopping tastes. At Cole Avenue pop in to the **Charles Hosmer Morse Museum** (see p119); its outstanding collection of Tiffany glass is a must-see. Follow this with a relaxing trip on the **Winter Park Scenic Boat Tour** (see p119), which departs from a dock on Morse Street, just a 15-minute walk away. On your return, lunch options are plentiful, but if the weather is good, grab one of the sidewalk tables at the **Park Plaza Gardens** (see p122) for some good food and people-watching.

Afternoon

After lunch, continue south on Park Avenue to Rollins College, home of the excellent **Cornell Fine Arts Museum** (see p119) and spend the rest of the afternoon enjoying this small but excellent collection.

Evening

Then, it's a ten-minute car ride north to Maitland's **Enzian Theater** where you can settle in to enjoy the latest in US and foreign independent films with a bottle of wine and a cheese plate. End the day at the bustling **Brio Tuscan Grille** (see p123) just a few minutes south by car, savoring a pink cosmopolitan or a gorgonzola-encrusted steak.

Around Town – Winter Park, Maitland, & Eatonville

Left **Houston's** Right **Fiddler's Green**

🔟 Bars & Nightspots

Brio Tuscan Grille
The trendy grill at Brio is wildly popular, but a lot of people come just to hang out at the bar here. Cocktails flow fast and furious for a crowd of well-heeled locals. *See p123.*

Dexter's of Winter Park
Home to a serious collection of wines, this branch of Dexter's is more upscale than Downtown's, except on Thursdays when there's a band playing classic rock. ● *558 W. New England Ave • Map L4 • 407-629-1150*

Fiddler's Green
This energetic Irish pub has darts, music, and a full selection of draft beers and stouts. It stays open until 2am most nights, making it popular for a last round. The food is good, too. *See p123.*

Park Plaza Gardens
With tables spilling out onto Park Avenue, this café bar is the bar of choice for an older set, who enjoy a cigar and glass of wine. *See p123.*

Ballard & Corum
This is a bakery that doubles as a bar by night. The bakery is open six days (not Sundays) to 5pm, and the bar opens at 6pm Thursday to Saturday. ● *535 W. New England Ave • Map L4 • 407-539-1711*

Copper Rocket Pub
With a small stage that hosts jazz jams to psycho rock, Copper Rocket is the only true music bar in the area. Microbrews and import beers fuel the young audience. ● *106 Lake Ave • Map K3 • 407-645-0069*

Circa 1926
There's something for everyone at this stylish nightspot – a trendy bar and lounge upstairs, a sleek bar with live piano music up front, and two elegant dining rooms. *See p123.*

Houston's
At one of Winter Park's top spots in which to be seen the draw may be the generous glasses of wine, or the fact that the entire restaurant menu is available at the bar. *See p123.*

Miller's Winter Park Ale House
Popular with the locals who go for a good brew and to watch sport on the plasma screen, the Ale House also serves reasonably priced meals and cocktails. ● *101 University Park Dr • Map L4 • 407-671-1011*

Mellow Mushroom Beer Bar
This friendly, low-key bar offers an extraordinary selection of beers. It serves very good pizza as well. ● *2015 Aloma Ave • Map L5 • 407-657-7755*

Price Categories

For a three-course meal for one with a glass of house wine, and all unavoidable extra charges including tax.

$	under $20
$$	$20–$30
$$$	$30–$45
$$$$	$45–$60
$$$$$	over $60

Brio Tuscan Grille

🔟 Cafés & Restaurants

Around Town – Winter Park, Maitland, & Eatonville

Circa 1926
The inventive chef pairs Italian-influenced appetizers with French entrées at this stylish restaurant with a relaxing atmosphere. 🟉 358 N. Park Ave • Map L4 • 407-637-5903 • $$$$

Panullo's Italian Restaurant
From the crispy calamari to the lobster ravioli, this reasonably priced neighborhood eatery is a great place to bring the whole family. 🟉 216 S. Park Ave • Map L4 • 407-629-7270 • $$

Park Plaza Gardens
The menu at this garden restaurant is regional Americana with a focus on seafood, such as blue crab cakes with mustard sauce. See p69. 🟉 319 S. Park Ave • Map L4 • 407-645-2475 • $$$$

Fiddler's Green
A wooden bar imported from Ireland, weekly folk bands, and authentic Gaelic dishes contribute to Fiddler's real Irish atmosphere. 🟉 544 W. Fairbanks Ave • Map L3 • 407-645-2050 • $$

Bubbalou's Bodacious BBQ
Smoked meat is the name of the game at this family joint. The sauces to put on range from mild to killer hot. 🟉 1471 Lee Rd • Map K3 • 407-628-1212 • No vegetarian dishes • No DA • $

Briarpatch Restaurant
Winter Park's homey breakfast landmark is known for big omelets and fresh fruit platters, but the creative, healthy American menu will make you consider returning for lunch. 🟉 252 N. Park Ave • Map L4 • 407-628-8651 • $$

Houston's
Here, various cuts of meat are chopped thick and cooked on a wood-burning grill. Portions are huge, particularly the salads and desserts. There are also seafood options. 🟉 215 S. Orlando Ave • Map L3 • 407-740-4005 • $$$$

Brio Tuscan Grille
This local favorite has a huge dining room that buzzes with chatter and the sizzle of grilling in the open kitchen. 🟉 480 N. Orlando Ave • Map L3 • 407-622-5611 • $$$

Luma on Park
Superlative cuisine, a head-spinning wine list, and an ultra-hip environment can be found at Luma on Park, which throbs with beautiful people. 🟉 290 S. Park Ave • Map L4 • 407-599-4111 • No kids' menu • Dinner only • $$$$

Café de France
Despite the name, this eatery has an international menu served in an upbeat setting. 🟉 526 S. Park Ave • Map L4 • 407-647-1869 • No kids' menu • No vegetarian dishes • $$$$

Unless stated, all restaurants advise reservations, are non-smoking, take credit cards, have DA, kids' menus, A/C, and vegetarian dishes.

STREETSMART

ORLANDO'S TOP 10

Left **Monorail, Orlando International Airport** Right **Summer theme park crowds**

TOP 10 Things to Know Before You Go

1 Orlando International Airport

Serving more than 100 cities worldwide, and handling 31 million passengers a year, this is the city's busiest airport. Forty scheduled airlines use it: the major domestic carriers include Delta, American, Northwest, US Airways, America West, and Southwest. British Airways, Virgin Atlantic, Air Canada, Iberia, and Saudi Arabian Airlines are some of its international carriers. Check the website *(see p130)* for information and maps to make sure you don't spend more time there than you need to. The airport is located about a 30-minute drive from Walt Disney World – if traffic is good.

2 Orlando Sanford International

Orlando's second airport, used primarily by international flights, is around an hour's drive from the Disney resorts. It is far smaller (used by just 1.2 million passengers per year) and promises a less crowded, less hectic start to a vacation.

3 Orlando Executive Airport

Situated just three miles (5 km) from the city's business center, Orlando's original airport is today used by private charters for both business and pleasure travelers.

4 US Entry Requirements for Canadian Visitors

Canadians need a passport to travel to the US.

5 US Entry Requirements for Overseas Visitors

International visitors must register with the Electronic System for Travel Authorization (ESTA) well in advance of travel; this can be done online (http://esta.cbp.dhs.gov) or at a travel agents. Citizens from the UK, South Africa, Australia, New Zealand, and many European countries may visit for up to 90 days without a visa if they have a valid passport. Other nationals should apply for a visa from their local US consulate or embassy well before they travel. Visit www.state.gov for the latest information.

6 Arriving by Train & Bus

Two Greyhound bus terminals and four Amtrak rail stations (including Sanford's Auto train terminal) serve the Orlando area. Tickets are rarely much cheaper than those for equivalent journeys by air.

7 Consolidators & Packagers

Consolidators buy bulk airline seats (and sometimes rooms) to sell at cheaper prices. Try 800-FLY-CHEAP (800-359-2432; www.1800 flycheap.com). Packagers sell full or partial packages that can include flight, room, rental car, and theme park tickets. Some parks have their own; or try www.vacation packager.com. *Disney packages • 407-828-8101 • www.disneyworld.com SeaWorld packages • 407-351-3600 • http:// 4adventure.com/seaworld/ fla Universal packages • 407-224-7000 • www. universalorlando.com*

8 Beat the Crowds

Theme park crowds are thinnest from the second week in September to the third week in November, the first two weeks of December, mid-January to mid-March, and late April through the third week of May. Weekends are always busy.

9 Weather Wise

Heat and humidity can be oppressive in summer, when temperatures easily hit 90°F (32°C) and lightning is another summer threat. High pollen counts in spring can make life hell for allergy sufferers and hurricane season is from August to November.

10 Online Planning

USA Tourist (www. usatourist.com) has multilingual information on attractions, hotels, restaurants, and more. Search engines are also useful for planning a trip, while Map Quest (www.mapquest.com) can help you plan a route once you've arrived.

For useful addresses **See pp130–31**

Left **I-Ride Trolly** Center **Lynx Bus Stop** Right **Taxi**

🔟 Tips on Getting Around Orlando

Renting a Car
Most major car rental companies have offices at or near both major airports, as well as in town. Many also have shuttles serving the Amtrak and Greyhound stations. Most agencies offer special deals via their websites (see p130) or packagers. Local maps are provided, and staff can help plan the route to your hotel.

Navigating Orlando
The city's major north–south artery is Interstate Highway 4 (Hwy I-4), which connects the main tourist areas. The Beachline Expressway (Hwy 528) is an east–west tollway useful for reaching the Kennedy Space Center (see pp38–41). Most main roads suffer gridlock during rush hour (7–9am and 4–6pm daily).

Shuttle Options
Mears shuttle buses travel from Orlando International Airport to hotels (the price varies according to distance), and around the tourist areas, including the Kennedy Space Center. Quick Transportation offers the same service, and can carry up to six people but offers personalized pickup and takes you straight to your destination. ✪ *Mears* • 407-423-5566 • *www. mearstransportation.com* ✪ *Quick Transportation* • 407-354-2456 • *www. quicktransportation.com*

Hotel Shuttles
Some hotels offer an airport shuttle service, and many offer transport to and from theme parks and other attractions several times per day. The service is usually free of charge to the parks nearest them, or available for a small charge to get to the others. Inquire about services when booking or planning your vacation.

Taking a Taxi
Taxis can be an economical way to get around for groups of four or five people. The fares from Orlando International and Orlando Sanford International airports to Walt Disney World are around $55 and $110 (plus tip) respectively. Extra charges apply at nights, weekends, and on public holidays. Cabs are easily found at airports and major hotels – otherwise call (see p131), as they are not that easy to flag down in the street.

The Disney Transportation System
Disney's free transportation system (monorail, buses, water taxis, and ferries) means you can save money by not renting a car and paying for gas and parking. It's best for guests who will spend most of their time with Mickey. But the circuits are set in stone and it can sometimes take an hour to reach some destinations in the resort.

The I-Ride Trolley
This service is a convenient and cheap way to get from A to B along the Universal, SeaWorld, and International Drive corridor. Trolleys run every 15 minutes, 7am–11:30pm daily, and make 54 stops. Exact change is required.
✪ 407-248-9590
• www.iridetrolley.com

Lynx Buses
Other than walking or cycling, Orlando's public bus system is the least popular way for most visitors to get around: buses can be frustratingly slow. Bus stops are marked with a paw print. Exact change is required. ✪ *Lynx Downtown Bus Terminal*
• 78 W. Central Blvd
• 407-841-8240
• www.golynx.com

Hiring a Limo
The least economical but most luxurious way to get around is by limousine – an option for travelers who want to be pampered and who have deeper pockets.
✪ *Advantage Limousine Service* • 407-438-8888
• www.advantagelimo.com

Walking
This is one of the USA's most dangerous cities for pedestrians: apart from wide highways with fast-moving traffic, there's a shortage of sidewalks, crosswalks, and street lights.

Left **Newspaper vending machines** Right **Kissimmee Convention & Visitors Bureau**

TOP 10 Sources of Information

1 Orlando/Orange Co. Convention & Visitors Bureau

Billed as "the official destination marketing organization for Orlando", this group provides an impressively comprehensive service. Their website is outstanding, offering up-to-date information and on-line booking, while the office can provide maps, directions, and answer questions. ⊗ *8723 International Dr • 407-363-5872 • www. orlandoinfo.com*

2 Kissimmee/St. Cloud Convention & Visitors Bureau

Focusing on the south of Orlando, this organization offers an excellent website and an office stocked with hundreds of brochures from area attractions. ⊗ *1925 E. Irlo Bronson Hwy. • 407-847-5000 • www.floridakiss.com*

3 Orlando Sentinel

The sole major daily newspaper in town is notoriously conservative in political matters, but the Friday edition carries an excellent arts and events section called the Calendar. There's an on-line version too (www. orlandosentinel.com).

4 Orlando Weekly

O-Town's primary "alternative" paper is this free weekly, which carries excellent and extremely detailed club and arts listings. The columnists –

all good, some hilarious – know the local scene intimately. The paper's website (www.orlando weekly.com) offers all the articles as well as terrific search capabilities for movie and music listings. The paper is available in restaurants, shops, clubs, convenience stores, and street boxes all over town.

5 Watermark

This free bi-weekly newspaper is the voice of Orlando's extensive gay and lesbian community. Not particularly radical, it offers splendid coverage of arts and events and is the best resource for clubs, shows, and more for the community. Available at gay-friendly businesses and in street boxes. There's also an on-line version: www.water markonline.com.

6 Gay, Lesbian, & Bisexual Community Services of Central Florida

This "lesbigay" community center is the city's clearinghouse for gay community information, ranging from art openings to health alerts. The organization regularly sponsors a variety of cultural events around town. ⊗ *407-228-8272 • www.glbcc.org*

7 News Channel 13

This is Orlando's own version of CNN – a 24-hour cable news channel devoted to O-Town. It is

probably most useful to visitors for the weather update that runs every ten minutes (1:01, 1:11, 1:21, etc). ⊗ *Only available on TVs subscribed to Time Warner Cable*

8 WTKS 104.1-FM

As well as national media superstar and controversial presenter Howard Stern's syndicated show (weekday mornings), the schedule of this radio station is filled with local talk radio personalities. All offer an interesting window into Orlando's current state of mind.

9 WMFE 90.7-FM

The area's best public radio station is best known for intelligent hourly news. The rest of the day offers light classical music – useful for calming down frustrated drivers in I-4 road jams *(see p140)* – with weekends turned over to syndicated public radio shows.

10 Brochure Racks

Virtually every hotel, restaurant, and attraction offers a huge lobby display packed with brochures and tourist guides covering almost all the hotels, restaurants, and smaller attractions in the area. Besides the maps and general information, discount coupons are common in these publications, so they're worth picking up *(see p133).*

Camp SeaWorld

ⓉⓄ10 Behind-the-Scenes Tours

1 Backstage Magic
Disney's most complete but expensive tour is ideal for guests who have to know what makes things tick. The seven-hour visit explores the inner workings of Epcot technology, the art of animation at Disney Hollywood Studios, and the Magic Kingdom's underground operations hub. ✆ 407-939-8687 • Max 20 people, 16 yrs & over • 9am Mon–Fri

2 Keys to the Kingdom
A useful, four-to-five hour Magic Kingdom taster tour for guests who'd like to see what's on offer before they really get started. It gives a basic park orientation as well as a glimpse of some of the usually hidden high-tech magic. ✆ 407-939-8687 • Min age 16 yrs • Cost does not include park adm • 8:30am, 9:30am, 10am, & 1:30pm daily

3 Hidden Treasures of World Showcase
This three-hour tour offers a closer view than most park guests get of Epcot's multi-cultural treasures. ✆ 407-939-8687 • Max 20 people, min age 16 yrs • Cost does not include park adm • 9am Tue & Thu

4 Family Magic Tour
Kids love this two-hour scavenger hunt in Disney World's most child-friendly park, the Magic Kingdom. Characters also meet guests at the end of the tour. ✆ 407-939-8687 • Cost does not include park adm • 9:30 & 11:30am daily

5 VIP Tours
Both Disney and Universal offer VIP tours – at a price. Disney's lets guests create their own itinerary, which could take in one or more parks, meals, golf, spa treatments, and more. The tour includes reserved show seating but not front-of-the-line access to rides. Universal's five-hour fixed tour offers line-cutting privileges at up to eight rides and shows. ✆ Disney • 407-560-4033 • Up to 10 people per tour, 5-hour min ✆ Universal • 407-363-8000 • 10am & noon daily

6 Scenic/Eco Lake Tours
See the real Florida and its wildlife during a fascinating one-hour narrated tour in a 24-ft (7-m) pontoon boat. Fishing and private charters, as well as island and gator tours, are also available. ✆ 101 Lakeshore Blvd, Kissimmee • 800-244-9105, 407-908-5688 • www.fishingchartersinc.com

7 Yuletide Fantasy
It's hard to beat Disney's Christmas celebration. This three-hour tour gives guests a front-row look at how the four theme parks and Fort Wilderness Lodge resort are transformed into a winter wonderland.

Highlights include a candlelight procession and Epcot's massed choir. This tour is guaranteed to get visitors into the holiday spirit. ✆ 407-824-4321 • Park adm not required • 9am Mon–Sat Nov 30–Dec 24

8 Camp SeaWorld
During the summer, SeaWorld offers several day programs to suit all budgets. The camps are divided by age from pre-school through 8th grade (13 yrs) and are designed to help kids better understand the marine animal world. There are family sleep-over programs, too. ✆ 407-370-1380 • Jun–Aug

9 To the Rescue
This is an hour-long tour of SeaWorld's rescue and rehabilitation efforts (see p31). The tour goes through critical-care and quarantine areas, as well as laboratories and surgical units. ✆ 407-351-3600 • Cost does not include park adm • Times vary

10 Polar Expedition Guided Tour
SeaWorld's cold-climate creatures, including beluga whales and the polar bears Klondike and Snow, are the stars of this hour-long tour. It finishes at the avian research facility where guests get to meet and touch a penguin. ✆ 407-351-3600 • Cost does not include park adm • Times vary

Tours should be reserved at least one month in advance.

Useful Addresses

Tourist Information

Orlando/Orange County Convention & Visitors' Bureau
6700 Forum Dr, Ste 100 (DO) • 407-363-5800

Tourist Information Center
8723 International Dr (I-D) • 407-363-5872

Websites

Citysearch
orlando.citysearch.com

Digital City
www.digitalcity.com/orlando

Go2Orlando
www.go2orlando.com

FLAUSA
www.flausa.com

Inside Central Florida
www.icflorida.com

Themeparks.com
www.themeparks.com

Airports

Orlando Executive Airport (ORL)
501 Herndon Ave • 407-894-9831 • www.fen.state.fl.us/goaa/oea.html

Orlando International Airport (MCO)
1 Airport Blvd • 407-825-2001 • www.orlando airports.net

Orlando Sanford Airport (SFB)
2 Red Cleveland Blvd, Sanford • 407-322-7771 • www.osi-airport.com

American Automobile Association (AAA)

4300 E.Colonial Dr • 407-894-3333 • www.aaa.com

Amtrak Train Stations

1400 Sligh Blvd (DO) • 407-843-7611 • www.amtrak.com

150 W. Morse Blvd (WP) • 407-645-5055 • www.amtrak.com

600 Persimmon Ave (Sanford) • 407-330-9770 • www.amtrak.com

111 Dakin St (K) • 407-933-1170 • www.amtrak.com

Greyhound Bus Terminals

103 E. Dakin Ave (K) • 888-332-6363; 407-847-3911 • www.greyhound.com

555 N. John Young Pkwy (DO) • 888-332-6363; 407-292-3424 • www.greyhound.com

Car Rental

Alamo
8200 McCoy Rd • 800-462-5266 • www.goalamo.com

Avis
8600 Hangar Blvd • 800-230-4898 • www.avis.com

Budget
8855 Rent A Car Rd • 800-527-7000 • www.budget.com

Dollar
8735 Rent A Car Rd • 800-800-4000 • www.dollarcar.com

Enterprise
7652 Narcoossee Rd • 800-325-8007 • www.enterprise.com

Hertz
5601 Butler National Dr • 800-654-3131 • www.hertz.com

National
8350 Hangar Blvd • 800-227-7368 • www.national car.com

Thrifty
5600 Butler National Dr • 800-847-4389 • www.thrifty.com

Banks

AmSouth Bank
111 N. Orange Ave (DO) • 800-267-6884

5401 S. Kirkman Rd (WDW) • 800-267-6884

Bank of America
390 N. Orange Ave (DO) • 800-432-1000

SunTrust
7625 Sand Lake Rd (I-D) • 407-762-4786

3357 Vine St (K) • 800-786-8787

400 S. Park Ave (WP) • 800-786-8787

Wachovia
7204 Sand Lake Rd (I-D) • 800-922-4684

Washington Mutual
7674 Dr. Phillips Blvd (WDW) • 800-788-7000

Credit Cards

American Express
800-528-4800 • www.american express.com

Diners Club
800-234-6377 • www.dinersclub.com

Discover
800-347-2683 • www.discovercard.com

MasterCard
800-826-2181 • www.mastercard.com

Key: DO: Downtown; I-D: International Drive; K: Kissimmee; WDW: Walt Disney World & Lake Buena Vista; WP: Winter Park & Maitland

Visa
800-336-8472
• www.visa.com

Hospitals

Celebration Health
400 Celebration Pl (WDW)
• 407-303-4000

Florida Hospital
7727 Lake Underhill Rd (DO) • 407-303-8110

2450 N. Orange Blossom Trail (K) • 407-846-4343

Sand Lake Hospital
9400 Turkey Lake Rd (I-D)
• 407-351-8550

Winter Park Memorial Hospital
200 N. Lakemont Ave (WP)
• 407-646-7000

Walk-In Clinics

Centra Care Walk-In Clinic
12500 S. Apopka Vineland Rd (WDW)
• 407-239-7777

4320 W. Vine St (K)
• 407-390-1888

ExpressCare
2700 Professional Pkwy (DO) • 407-656-2055

Orlando Regional Walk-In Medical Care
9400 Turkey Lake Rd (I-D)
• 407-841-5111

WinterPark Family Practice
2830 Casa Aloma Way (WP)
• 407-678-5554

24-hour Pharmacy

CVS Pharmacy
1205 W. Vine St (K)
• 407-847-5174

3502 Edgewater Dr (DO)
• 407-245-1001

Walgreens
2420 E. Colonial Dr (DO)
• 407-894-5361

6201 International Dr (I-D) • 407-345-8311

13502 Apopka Vineland Rd (WDW) • 407-827-1000

Dentists

Advanced Dental Care
4020 S. Semoran Blvd (DO)
• 407-277-5787

Coast Dental
2200 E. Irlo Bronson Memorial Hwy (K)
• 407-935-1772

2951 Vineland Rd (WDW)
• 407-396-1288

Greenburg Dental Associates
4780 S. Kirkman Rd (I-D)
• 407-292-7373

7762 University Blvd (WP)
• 407-671-0001

Help Lines

Central Florida Helpline
407-333-9028

Society for Accessible Travel & Hospitality
212-447-7284

Help Now of Osceola
407-847-8562

Internet Access

Fedex Kinko's
9800 International Dr (I-D)
• 407-363-2831
• www.fedex.com

2145 Aloma Ave (WP)
• 407-677-9950
• www.fedex.com

4350 W. Vine St (K)
• 407-396-2923
• www.fedex.com

Orlando Public Library
101 E. Central Blvd (DO)
• 407-835-7323

South Orange Library
1702 Deerfield Blvd (WDW)
• 407-858-4779

Post Offices

46 E. Robinson St (DO)
• 407-425-6464

10450 Turkey Lake Rd (I-D)
• 800-275-8777

2600 Michigan Ave (K)
• 407-846-0999

12133 S. Apopka Vineland Rd (WDW) • 407-238-0223

300 N. New York Ave (WP)
• 407-647-6807

Police

City of Kissimmee Police
8 N. Stewart Ave (K) • 407-846-3333 • Emergency: 911

City of Orlando Police
100 S. Hughey Ave (I-D)
• 321-235-5300
• Emergency: 911

Orange County Sherriff
2500 W. Colonial Dr (DO)
• 407-836-4357
• Emergency: 911

Osceola County Sheriff
400 Simpson Rd (K) • 407-348-2222 • Emergency: 911

Winter Park Police
401 S. Park Ave (WP) • 407-644-1313 • Emergency: 911

Consulates

Australia
2103 Coral Way, Ste 108, Miami • 305-858-7633

Canada
200 S. Biscayne Blvd, Ste 1600, Miami • 305-579-1600

Japan
80 S.W. 8th St, Miami
• 305-530-9090

United Kingdom
200 S. Orange Ave, Ste 2110, Orlando • 407-254-3300

For more on tourist information **See p128**

Left **Fastpass ticket outlet** Center **Souvenirs from SeaWorld** Right **Disney memorabilia**

TOP 10 Tips on Shopping & Tickets

1 Shopping Hours
Shops in theme parks keep the same hours as the parks. Malls and outlets are usually open from 9 or 10am until 9pm Monday to Saturday and at least noon to 6pm on Sunday. Shops outside the main tourist areas tend to open from 9am to 5pm Monday through Saturday.

2 Sales Tax
With the exception of groceries and some medications, all purchases in Orlando are subject to a 6 per cent state and local sales tax.

3 Sales
Look for winter-wear bargains from March through April, and summer bargains from August to October as the seasonal stock changes. In August, with the approach of the new school year, there are good buys on kids' clothes. The day after Thanksgiving is the biggest shopping day of the year, with huge pre-Christmas sales attracting hordes of shoppers.

4 Outlets
Outlet stores sell last season's fashions at discounted prices. Shoppers who know the suggested retail prices of the goods they seek will be able to tell what is – and what isn't – a bargain. Some stores promise as much as 75 per cent discount and some actually deliver.

Others don't. The big players here are the Orlando Premium and Prime outlets *(see p66)*.

5 Gifts & Souvenirs
Apart from cheap T-shirts, stuffed animals, and baseball caps, Orlando does have some more original souvenirs. These include Florida oranges, alligator meat and leather products, and manatee memorabilia.

6 Shipping Home
If you have bought more souvenirs than you can carry home, why not ship them? Disney and Universal parks, resorts, and shops can make the arrangements, usually via United Parcel Service (UPS). Do-it-yourselfers must take their packages to UPS (call 1-800-742-5877 for the nearest center) or the US Postal Service (1-800-275-8777).

7 Buy Theme Park Tickets Online
Disney (www.disneyworld.com) allows guests to buy tickets online, saving on time waiting in line, but they must be picked up in person. Universal (www.universalorlando.com) mails online tickets to buyers; buy at least five weeks in advance. SeaWorld's online service (www.seaworld.com) lets buyers print out their tickets and, when they arrive at the park, go straight to the turnstiles, where they are verified.

8 Multi-Day & Multi-Park Passes
Disney's Park Hopper and Park Hopper Plus tickets are valid for four to seven days. Both include unlimited entry to the four parks; the Park Hopper Plus tickets also include entry to other Disney attractions. The discounts aren't great, but you save time waiting in line. Universal (which also offers a separate two-to-three-day pass for Universal Parks only), SeaWorld, Wet 'n Wild, and Tampa's Busch Gardens have joined up to offer the unlimited access, 14-day FlexTicket.

9 Cutting in Line
Disney (FastPass) and Universal and SeaWorld (Express) offer a system that cuts out the long wait for the most popular rides and shows. Just slide your ticket through the turnstile to get an allocated time for your visit. When it's time, simply go to the particular attraction's designated entrance to take your place.

10 Concierge Desks
Most upscale and some moderately priced hotels have concierge desks in the lobby. They're great places to make restaurant reservations or buy tickets for theme parks and other attractions. They don't give discounts, but most do offer the convenience of waiting in a short line as opposed to a long one in the parks.

Left **Hotel shuttle bus** Right **Leaflets in a hotel lobby**

Tips for the Budget Conscious

The Magicard
The Orlando/Orange County CVB's *(see p128)* Magicard offers $500 worth of discounts on accommodation, car rentals, attractions, meals, shopping, and more. It also offers deals that combine rooms with attraction and theme park tickets. Each card is valid for up to six people, and it's free. Allow four weeks for delivery.
407-363-5872 • www. orlandoinfo.com

Hotel Handouts
Many hotels and motels offer freebies such as continental breakfasts, evening hors d'oeuvres, and news-papers. Their coupon racks are stuffed with two-for-one and other special deals on meals and attractions. For those without a car, most hotels have free or low-fee shuttle services to the parks.

Newspaper Coupons
The Sunday travel sec-tions in many major US newspapers lure people to Orlando with offers of coupons, cheap fares, and package deals. Once here, read the Orlando Sentinel (especially Friday's Calendar section), as well as the free papers available on street corners and in hotel lobbies, all of which feature lots of discounts and offers. *See p128.*

Rooms with Cooking Facilities
Travelers can save big by booking a room with a kitchen, kitchenette, or even just a microwave and refrigerator. Apart from Walt Disney World properties, most accom-modation is close to supermarkets or delica-tessens, some of which deliver for a small fee.

Pack a Snack & Water
Theme-park prices for refreshments are 30–50 per cent higher than what people pay outside the parks. The parks prohibit coolers (containers for keeping food and drink cool), but guests can bring their own bottled water and snacks. Some parks have fountains, but the water in Central Florida does not taste particularly sweet.

Eat Big Early & Late
It's often unnecessary to eat three big meals a day, particularly in the hottest months of the year. If you want to skip, or go light on, lunch, you can eat well – and cheaply – before and after your theme-park visit by having a low-priced, all-you-can-eat, buffet breakfast and an early-bird dinner *(see p134).*

Fast Food & Family Restaurants
Orlando is chock-full of fast-food outlets. The city also has an abundance of very well-priced family restaurants *(see pp70–71).* Most have kids' menus, which can be even cheaper at lunchtime.

OTIX!
The cultural crowd isn't left out of the dis-count mix. The city's CVB *(see p128)* regularly has half-price tickets, includ-ing those for opera, ballet, music, and theater. The tickets are for same-day performances, and while information is available by phone, the tickets must be picked up in person. 407-872-2382

Staying at Disney on the Cheap
People who really want to stay at Disney World, but can't afford the prices, can find the cheapest rates at the All-Star resorts *(see p142).* Rack rates (those anyone can get without a discount) are extraordinarily reasonable and kids also stay free. But be warned: rooms at these "value" resorts are very cramped.

Gas for Renters
Never buy gas for a rental car from the car hire company itself. Some of their offers sound entic-ing, especially those offer-ing cheaper gas if you buy up front rather than when the car is returned. Most of the time, fuel prices are cheaper – sometimes much cheaper – around town.

Sign up for DK's email newsletter on traveldk.com

Buffet breakfast

TOP 10 Tips on Eating & Drinking

1 Disney World's Priority Seating

Disney restaurants don't take reservations. In their place, they use what they call a priority seating system. Callers are given a time to arrive; when they turn up, the next available table is given to them (as opposed to a table being held open). Note that all restaurants inside Disney parks, except Animal Kingdom's Rainforest Café, require park admission.

2 Reservations

Whenever restaurants accept reservations, make them – especially in the main tourist areas of I-Drive, Lake Buena Vista, and along Irlo Bronson Memorial Highway in Kissimmee. Not having a reservation can mean waiting two hours for a table during prime dining time, usually 6–8:30pm. Some restaurants refuse to seat diners who have not reserved in advance and upscale eateries may be unable to accommodate you unless you reserve far ahead.

3 Gratuities

Wait staff expect a tip of at least 15 per cent. Those who are particularly helpful may deserve 20 per cent; you may want to give just 10 per cent to those who aren't. Some restaurants now add tips to the bill, so check before paying.

4 Smoking

New laws passed in Florida mean that all restaurants are now non-smoking establishments. If you want to smoke while you drink, you have to find a bar where eating is only incidental to drinking. If you aren't sure, just smoke outside.

5 Buffet Breakfast Bargains

There are several modestly priced, all-you-can-eat breakfast buffets around town (especially on I-Drive and in Kissimmee). For a handful of dollars, you can fill your stomach and save money by eating a light lunch or skipping it altogether.

6 Early Birds

Some value restaurants offer cut-rate meals when business is slow, which is usually between 4pm and 6pm, Monday–Friday. These early-bird deals are usually advertised outside and are offered in the free coupon books found in hotel lobbies and tourist attractions. Many of these restaurants also offer 2-for-1 drink specials during these times.

7 Lunch Menus vs Dinner Menus

Many upscale restaurants are not only hard to get in to at dinnertime, but the menus are very expensive. The lunch menu might have fewer options, and portions tend to be a little less generous, but the prices are lower. To save money – and your digestive system – consider eating your main meal at mid-day and eating lighter at night.

8 Special Diets

Some restaurants that don't normally offer meat- and seafood-free options are happy to prepare vegetarian dishes, with some prior warning. Disney restaurants go one step further and provide for a variety of other dietary needs, including kosher, fat- or sugar-free, plus lactose intolerance and allergies. Give 24 hours' notice. ✆ 407-824-2222 (407-939-3463 if staying on Disney property).

9 Happy Hours

Many bars (and restaurants) have happy hours, usually from 4–7pm, when drinks are often two for the price of one. They sometimes serve special hors d'oeuvres as well.

10 Hotel Mini Bars

Put bluntly, these are rip-offs. Years ago, inventive guests drank the good stuff and refilled the bottles with cheap brands. So now the mini bars have a sensor: remove the bottle for 10 seconds and you get charged – a lot – for it.

Left **Sun protection** Rght **24-hour pharmacy**

🔟 Health Tips

1 Heat, Sun & Insects
Heat and humidity during the summer season (June to mid-September) can cause dehydration, so be sure to drink at least two quarts (two liters) of fluids (preferably water) each day, and wear a wide-brimmed hat and airy clothes. Not only does too much sun result in nasty burns, but it can also cause sun poisoning. Use a sunscreen with a high protection factor. And as much as Disney and Universal want to erase bloodsucking flies and mosquitoes, they can't, so remember to use insect repellent in summer.

2 911
This is the number to call for emergency health matters and for immediate police or fire assistance.

3 Hospitals & First Aid
Ask at your hotel or resort reception for the nearest hospital. Make sure you have some kind of insurance, otherwise hospital costs can be crippling. All of the major parks have first-aid clinics for minor ailments.

4 Ask-A-Pharmacist
Most pharmacists are happy to give you first aid advice, as well as advice regarding how to take medicines. Most pharmacies are not open 24 hours, but pharmacists will usually give advice over the phone so call a Walgreens or a CVS Pharmacy, which are usually open 24 hours. See p131.

5 In-Room Medical Care
House calls are a thing of the past in most US cities, but the tourist areas in Orlando have two services that make house and hotel-room calls. Doctors on Call Service and Centra Care In-Room Services cover most of the areas from Downtown south to Disney and Kissimmee.
🕾 *Doctors on Call Service • 407-399-3627* 🕾 *Centra Care In-Room Services • 407-238-2000*

6 Centra Care Walk-In Clinics
Centra Care (affiliated with the Florida Hospital) has walk-in clinics scattered throughout Orange, Seminole, and Osceola counties *(see p131)*. These clinics can handle minor emergencies (broken limbs, cuts requiring stitches, and fevers), but not life-threatening situations, for which you should call 911.

7 24-Hour Pharmacies
Several drug stores sell over-the-counter and prescription drugs around the clock *(see p131)*. Additional pharmacies, with regular hours, are listed in the Yellow Pages.

8 Dental Referral Service
This nationwide, toll-free service helps people to find the nearest suitable dentist. The telephones are answered 8am–8pm Monday–Friday; the automated answering service informs callers of the website then puts them on hold to speak to an operator. Those who prefer to choose for themselves, or anyone needing 24-hour aid, should use the Yellow Pages *(or see p131)*. 🕾 *888-343-3440 800-511-8663 • www.dentalreferral.com*

9 Poison Control
This 24-hour hotline can and has saved lives. Operators can help deal with a problem, summon rescuers, and answer questions. But, don't overlook 911 for any emergency situation. 🕾 *800-222-1222.*

10 Florida Tourism Industry Marketing Corp
While it shouldn't be used for emergencies, this tourism-funded group can provide basic information about medical services and assistance throughout the state. It also has a range of other services, including assistance with lost credit cards and documents, help with accidents, directions, and more. Operators can help in more than 150 languages. 🕾 *800-647-9284*

Left **ATM machine** Right **Quarters (25¢) & pennies (1¢)**

Communications & Money Tips

Making Phone Calls

Orlando's numbers have 10 digits – the area code (Central Florida's is 407), plus the seven-digit number. If calling a number with a different area (or toll-free) code, dial 1 before the code and phone number. To make calls overseas, consider buying a phone card.

Internet Access

Internet cafes *(see p131)* offer email and internet services for varying prices. Public libraries offer free access to the internet.

Languages

Disney, Universal, and larger hotels have multilingual staff who speak Spanish, French, German, and, in some cases, Dutch, Japanese, and other languages. They also have information printed in these languages. The Orlando/ Orange County Convention & Visitors Bureau and USA Tourist have multilingual websites.
❂ www.orlandoinfo.com
❂ www.usatourist.com

Post Offices

The United States Postal Service (USPS) has five post offices in the Orlando area. Opening hours vary, but they are usually 9am to 5pm weekdays, although some open Saturday mornings as well. Drugstores and

hotels often sell stamps, but they are slightly more expensive than those sold at post offices. Mailboxes, which are blue, are on most main streets and in hotels. Most major hotels also have daily collection services.

Credit Cards & Traveler's Checks

Most hotels, restaurants, attractions, and shops accept American Express, Diners Club, Discover, MasterCard, and Visa credit cards. Some also take Carte Blanche and JCB cards. US dollar denominations of American Express, Thomas Cook, and Visa traveler's checks are widely accepted with ID.

Currency & Exchanges

Dollar notes come in $1, $5, $10, $20, $50, and $100 bills. Coins in circulation are of 1 cent, 5 cents (a nickel), 10 cents (a dime), and 25 cents (a quarter) value. One-dollar and 50 cent coins exist but are very rare. Currency exchanges are based at all the airports, major branches of banks, and near guest services or guest relations in all major theme parks.

ATMs

Automatic Teller Machines (ATMs) are located at almost all bank branches, in all major theme parks, major shopping malls, some hotels,

and at airports. Most also accept withdrawals on American Express, MasterCard, and Visa credit cards. There is a $1.50 to $3 advance charge for cards not affiliated to that particular bank. It's often cheaper to use a debit card, but not all debit systems are supported by US banks; check the symbols on the ATM to see if yours is one that is accepted.

Bank Opening Hours

Most Central Florida banks are open 9am to 4pm weekdays (to 6pm on Friday). A few branches also open Saturday mornings. Most have ATMs with 24-hour access.

Western Union

International money transfers can be sent to more than 101,000 Western Union agents and offices in 187 countries. They can also arrange international telegrams.
❂ 1-800-325-6000

Taxes

The USA doesn't have a national sales tax. Instead, individual states and counties set the rate of sales tax. Florida levies a six per cent state, or state and local tax, on everything except groceries and certain medicines. Hotels also add an extra three to five per cent bed tax *(see p141)*.

Left **Valuables** Center **Orange County Sheriff's car** Right **Residential speed limit**

🔟 Safety Tips

1 On the Coast
Florida's beaches are usually well supervised by lifeguards, but still keep a close eye on young children and stick to areas where you can see the lifeguards. The same goes for rivers and pools.

2 Non-Emergency Numbers
Outside city limits, county sheriff's offices *(see p131)* are the primary police agencies: in Central Florida they are in Orange County, Osceola County, and Seminole County. For traffic and highway-related matters, call the Florida Highway Patrol. For coastal issues, see the Florida Marine Patrol. 🕾 *Florida Highway Patrol • 407-897-5959* 🕾 *Florida Marine Patrol • 321-383-2740*

3 Hurricanes
The coast is usually hit hardest by hurricanes, but Central Florida is also affected. Hurricane season is from August to November. If caught in one, stay inside, away from windows, and have lots of water, canned food, and a flashlight to hand. For more tips and up-to-date forecasts, see the Hurricane Weather Center. 🕾 *http://hurricane.weather center.com*

4 General Safety
Always keep car and hotel-room doors locked. Before driving, ask the rental-car company, your hotel's front-desk staff, or the Florida Tourism Industry Marketing Corporation *(see p135)* for the safest and most direct route to your destination. Don't let strangers change your currency, and when paying for anything, check you've been given the correct change before leaving the premises.

5 Valuables
Smart travelers leave valuables at home. If you do bring watches, jewelry, or other items of value, keep them in a hotel safe. The safes in hotel rooms should only be used for less valuable items. It's also advisable to carry credit cards or traveler's checks rather than large amounts of cash.

6 Stay in Populated, Well-Lit Areas
Orlando doesn't have the same crime rate as many cities, but it has its share of thieves who prey on the unsuspecting. At night, avoid badly lit areas (especially Downtown's westside, south of Colonial Drive), and at all times be wary of pickpockets.

7 Lost Children
Nothing frightens a parent or guardian more than turning away for a moment only to find their child gone. It happens every day in Orlando's theme parks. To help staff reunite familes, children under seven should wear tags with their name, hotel, and a contact number on it. When any member of your group gets lost, find a park employee for assistance.

8 Seat Belts
Florida law requires seat belts to be worn by the driver and all passengers. Children five years and under need a federally approved child restraint: for those under three years the restraint must be a child seat; children four through five years can use a child seat or a seat belt. A fine of at least $50 will be made for non-compliance.

9 Drinking & Driving
In a word: Don't. Florida strictly enforces this law. Violators risk time in jail if convicted of a drink-driving offense. Have a designated driver in the group, skip alcohol for the night, use public transport, or grab taxis. Police are known to survey bars to see who is drinking, then wait outside until drinkers get in a car to drive off, when they are tested.

10 Speed Limits
Speed limits on interstates, toll roads, and major highways range from 55 to 70 mph (88–112 kmph). On smaller highways, the limit is 45 mph (72 kmph), and in residential areas, it's 30 to 35 mph (48–56 kmph). Fines begin at $160, doubling if it's in a school or construction zone.

Left **Mobility products** Center **Disabled parking facility** Right **Mature travelers**

Tips for Seniors & Disabled People

1 Mature Travelers Guide

The Orlando/Orange County CVB's Mature Travelers Guide offers nearly $300 worth of discount coupons for seniors. It also reviews places that may appeal to them. ✆ 407-363-5872 • www.orlandoinfo.com

2 AARP

The AARP (American Association of Retired Persons) is America's most vocal group for the elderly, but it doesn't forget there's room for fun. The website's travel articles are available to the public, but only members find out about AARP's travel deals and discounts. Membership costs are minimal. ✆ 1-202-434-2277 • www.aarp.org

3 Elderhostel

This educational travel organization sends people 55 and over on courses (usually for a week) all over the world. The choice of courses in Orlando is astounding, from travel photography to politics and philosophy. Stay at retreats, hotels, or campsites. ✆ 1-877-426-8056 • www.elderhostel.org

4 Disney Grandkids & You Getaway

Knowing that a lot of seniors come to Orlando with their grandkids, Disney occasionally offers discounted packages. Most include three nights in a Disney hotel, multiple-day tickets to the parks, and a range of goodies for the kids, such as dolls and autograph books. ✆ 407-934-7639 • www.disneyworld.com

5 Yvonne's Property Management

This service leases more than 20 wheelchair-accessible houses and villas in Davenport, a 15 minute drive southwest of Disney. They have three to six bedrooms, two or three bathrooms, accessible showers, and equipped kitchens. Many have pools fitted with lifts. ✆ 1-863-424-0795 • www.villasinorlando.com

6 Walker Medical & Mobility Products

The local franchise for Walker Medical & Mobility Products rents wheelchairs and three-wheel rechargeable electric scooters, including ones for people weighing more than 375 lbs (170 kg). They all fit into Disney's transport vehicles and can be taken apart to fit into cars. The company delivers to local hotels and houses. ✆ 888-726-6837 • www.walkermobility.com

7 Disney for Disabled Guests

The free Guidebook for Guests with Disabilities details special needs services, including: accessibility in parks; Braille directory locations; special-needs parking; wheelchair and electric-cart rentals; audio tours; and translator units for the deaf. They are available at Guest Services in all the theme parks or at Disney hotels' front desks. ✆ 407-824-4321 • www.disneyworld.com

8 Universal for Disabled Guests

Universal's parks and hotels have the following services: audio guides; wheelchair and scooter rentals; and telecommunications devices for the deaf. A free booklet is available from Guest Relations at park entrances and resort front desks. ✆ 407-363-8000 • www.universalorlando.com

9 SeaWorld for Disabled Guests

SeaWorld provides a Braille guide, plus a written synopsis of its shows and telecommunications devices for the hearing impaired. Most of its rides and shows are accessible. It rents wheelchairs and scooters. A small guidebook is available at Guest Relations. ✆ 407-351-3600 • www.seaworld.com

10 Society for Accessible Travel & Hospitality

Members pay an annual subscription for access to a range of services, but non-members can get information on travel for the disabled (including specific hotels and attractions) for a small fee. ✆ 1-212-447-7284 • www.sath.org

Streetsmart

Left **Getting wet** Center **Kids' menu** Right **SeaWorld stroller rental**

🔟 Tips for Families

1 Name Tags & Reunion Places

It's very easy to get lost in crowded theme parks. If that happens, find a park employee (they're usually in uniform) and ask for help. Kids seven and under should wear tags bearing their name, hotel, and a contact number. Older kids and adults should pick a place inside the park to meet if they become separated.

2 Parent-Swaps

Height restrictions *(see below)* mean that some younger children may not be able to go on certain rides. The theme parks usually have a program that lets one parent ride while the other tends to the kids in a special waiting area. Then the second parent can go on the ride: it might not be so much fun riding by yourself but at least you don't have to wait in line again.

3 Stroller Rental & Baby Care

All the major theme parks offer stroller rental. There are also excellent nursing facilities, often with free formula provided. Diaper changing tables can be found in women's and some men's restrooms, and diapers are available free of charge at Universal's parks.

4 Breaks

Theme parks are tiring at any time of year, but excessively so in summer, when even standing in line can be exhausting. Plan regular breaks at air-conditioned venues (best visited around midday, when it's hottest outside), or "splash areas" *(see below)*.

5 Refreshments

Bring snacks for energy and don't forget water. The parks have a few drinking fountains, but bottled water is very expensive.

6 Getting Wet & Not Getting Wet

Take a change of clothes to the theme parks, if not for yourself then for the children. Apart from water rides where you might expect to get wet, kids enjoy running through "splash areas" to cool off, and drying off naturally might not be possible. A rain poncho is smart year round, since Florida has rainy spells in both summer and winter.

7 Theme Park Ride Restrictions

Disney parks tend to have few health and height restrictions, although Disney Hollywood Studios is a little limiting. Universal's parks can be more restrictive for younger kids, especially Islands of Adventure (with warnings on nine of the 13 major rides), but like Universal Studios, it has a dedicated kids' area. SeaWorld has height restrictions on a couple of rides, while at Discovery Cove, you must be at least six years old to swim with the dolphins. Non-swimmers can still join in, but obviously can't enjoy the full experience.

8 Children's Menus

Most of the more expensive and dressy restaurants discourage young diners either by failing to provide children's menus or with outright bans on anyone under 17 years of age. However, most restaurants have some kind of kids' menu, usually in the $4 to $6 range. Some also provide distractions such as crayons and coloring-in placemats.

9 Character Meals

Disney lures families with children to a dozen of their restaurants to charge exorbitant prices for eating breakfast, lunch, or dinner with humans dressed in Disney character costumes. Universal also has one "character" restaurant, and there are some similar set-ups outside of theme parks. *See p71.*

10 Kids Stay Free

Orlando is Kidsville. The little ones don't pay, but they're the reason adults do. Smart hoteliers let kids stay free. Most rooms have beds for four, so even if there are only two in the party, the extra beds are part of the deal.

Left **Rush hour on I-4** Right **Merritt Island National Wildlife Refuge**

Things to Avoid

1 Park Visits When School's Out

All the parks are packed during school breaks (late Jun–late Aug; late Dec–early Jan; mid-Feb, and Easter), since that's when locals hit the parks with their kids. Summer is the worst, since not only is it crowded, but it's also brutally hot. The least crowded months are November plus early and late February.

2 Theme Park Isolation

Don't spend every waking minute in Orlando's theme parks, because burn-out is inevitable. Make sure you take time to see Central Florida's natural attractions *(see pp82–5)*, smaller attractions *(see pp44–5)*, and museums *(see pp60–61)*.

3 Early Arrivals

It might seem smart to hit the theme parks as soon as they open, but it is not always the best plan. Kids who arrive early tend to collapse by 2pm and are a mess the rest of the day. Instead, take it easy in the morning and head for the parks in the afternoons and evenings. Temperatures are cooler and the parks take on a magical glow under the lights.

4 Inflexibility

Relax. It's a vacation. There are no prizes for those who joylessly cram

every single ride at their chosen theme park into one day. Make plans, but be flexible. Don't attempt to do everything on your list, and maybe save a few things for the next visit.

5 Big Meals In-Park

In general, theme-park food is bland and overpriced, so don't waste your main meal of the day on it. Instead, at Universal, check out the eateries on Citywalk *(see p105)*; while at Disney, visit one of the excellent resort dining options, where you'll find that high-end restaurants offer great value. Parks allow same-day re-entry on single tickets – just be sure to get your hand stamped before leaving.

6 Free and Discount Tickets

There are a lot of offers floating around Orlando that sound too good to be true. If someone promises free or heavily discounted tickets, ask "What's the catch?", especially if they're promising a Disney ticket. Most are timeshare salespeople trying to get you to "buy" a week's holiday for the next 20 years. In some cases they have legitimate tickets, but most of the time you have to endure hours of sales pitches. Usually, such properties are overpriced.

7 Wearing Skimpy Bathing Suits at Water Parks

Ladies should consider one-piece suits at water parks since most of the best rides can quickly rip off a bikini top. Alternatively, wear a T-shirt over the bikini for added protection. Guys, for reasons not necessary to elaborate upon here, should avoid Speedos altogether.

8 Public Transport

Lynx buses might appear to be everywhere, but don't set your schedule by them, especially for longer trips. They stop frequently, are notoriously slow, and are generally ignored by locals.

9 Downtown's Westside

The area of Downtown south of Colonial Drive and west of I-4 is not a particularly safe place to wander around. Avoid it. But if you are going to a destination here, including the Greyhound Bus station, call a cab.

10 Rush Hour on I-4

Sometimes called "Orlando's Parking Lot", I-4 can get very congested, particularly during evening rush hour (3–6:30pm), as attraction employees head home. Disney-generated traffic on I-4, between Lake Buena Vista and US Hwy 192, has a life of its own. Traffic jams there can occur around the clock.

Left **Family-friendly motel** Right **View from hotel room**

🔟 Accommodation Tips

Bed & Sales Taxes

Hotels have an assortment of hidden add-ons that can come as a surprise when you get the bill. Charges for the mini-bar and pay-per-view movies are always inflated. But the sales tax (see p132) and bed tax can really add to the bill. Orange County, including the theme parks, I–Drive, and downtown Orlando, adds five per cent bed tax; Osceola County, which includes Kissimmee, adds 6 per cent; and Seminole County, which includes Sanford (see p85), adds a 3 per cent tax. Don't forget to factor in these extras when determining your vacation budget.

Rack Rates

These are the rates no one should agree to pay for a room! They're the walk-in-and-ask rates anyone can get without a coupon or package, and without asking for a discount or special deal. They're used in this book to provide a guide price, but don't settle for them. Insist on a better deal – it is almost always possible.

Rooms with a View

Many properties charge more for a room that has a view of anything other than the parking lot or the building next door. Before you pay, consider how much time you will want to spend in your room.

The Pros of Staying with Mickey

The main benefits are proximity to the parks, access to the free Disney transportation system (see p127), preferred tee times at Disney golf courses (see pp54–5), extra hours in the parks, and an easy way to break up the day by returning to base for a midday nap or swim.

The Cons of Staying with Mickey

The main drawback is the cost. Rates at Disney World Resorts are about 30 per cent more than comparable accommodation on the outside.

Types of Accommodation

Orlando has almost 107,000 hotel rooms. Most tend to be functional budget options, but there are plenty of upscale choices, too, from lavish resorts to one-off B&Bs and boutique hotels.

Booking Services

In addition to making independent reservations or dealing directly with Disney or Universal resorts, vacationers can use reservations networks to book rooms. Central Reservation Service (CRS), Orlando. com, and Vacation Works are three of the more popular ones. 🔊 Walt Disney World • 407-828-8101 • www.disneyworld. com 🔊 Universal • 407-224-7000 • www. universalorlando.com 🔊 CRS • 407-740-6442 • www.crshotels.com 🔊 Orlando.com • 800-675-2636 • www.orlando.com 🔊 Vacation Works • www.vacationworks.com

Land-Sea Options

A different approach is to take a seven-day land-sea package that includes a stay at any one or more Disney resorts plus a Caribbean cruise. 🔊 Disney Cruise Line • 800-951-3532 • www.disneycruise.com

Family-Friendly Motels

Most Orlando properties go the extra mile to make sure kids are treated like royalty. In fact, most let kids under 17 stay free with accompanying adults. Holiday Inn Family Suites (see p145) and Holiday Inn Sunspree (see p145) offer more than the usual child-friendly amenities.

In-Room Calls

Don't use the in-room phone to make any calls without knowing the billing policy. Some hotels offer free local calls, while others charge double or more the 35¢ cost of using an outside pay phone. Some impose a $1-plus service charge whenever the phone is used (including for toll-free numbers), in addition to long-distance rates.

For accommodation listings **See pp142–9**

Portofino Bay Hotel, a replica of a real village in Italy

TOP 10 Disney & Universal Resorts

1 Disney's Grand Floridian Resort & Spa

Disney's top hotel is an opulent, early 20th-century New England-style resort. Expect a ragtime mood and intimate rooms that promise romance and great views. The resort also has a full spa, health club, and tennis courts. ✆ 4401 Floridian Way • Map F1 • 407-824-3000 • www. disneyworld.com • $$$$

2 Disney's Board-Walk Inn & Villas

This re-created 1940s seaside village is Disney's smallest deluxe hotel. The rooms are delightfully quaint; if you want more space, villas are available too. It is ideally located for all the facilities and buzz of the BoardWalk. ✆ 2101 N. Epcot Resorts Blvd • Map G2 • 407-939-5100; www.disneyworld. com • $$$$

3 Portofino Bay Hotel

This Universal resort is a replica of Italy's Portofino village, right down to the boats and "fishermen" in the harbor. The rooms are spacious and feature luxe bed linen. The gelati (ice cream) machines by the pool are another nice touch. Guests get to skip the line for rides and shows at Universal's parks. ✆ 5601 Universal Blvd • Map T1 • 407-503-1000 • www.universal orlando.com • $$$$

4 Walt Disney World Dolphin

This Sheraton resort is on Disney property so offers some Disney perks, such as use of the free transportation system (see p127). The 27-floor pyramid contains outsize sculptures, a waterfall, plus more than 1,500 suites and rooms. ✆ 1500 Epcot Resorts Blvd • Map G2 • 407-934-4000 • www. swandolphin.com • $$$$

5 Walt Disney World Swan

With two 46-ft (14-m) swans gracing its roof, this hotel is hard to miss. The beach-themed rooms are a little smaller than at its sister hotel, the Dolphin, but Swan guests share some of the facilities and perks of the Dolphin, including a spa. ✆ 1200 Epcot Resorts Blvd • Map G2 • 407-934-3000 • www.swandolphin.com • $$$$

6 Disney's Yacht Club Resort

The theme here is New England yacht club. Some of the 630 nautical-style rooms have views over a lake. Guests can walk to Epcot in about 10 minutes. ✆ 1700 Epcot Resorts Blvd • Map G2 • 407-934-7000 • www. disneyworld.com • $$$$

7 Disney's Wilder-ness Lodge

Live oaks and yellow pines surround this lovely wooded resort, modeled on the Yosemite Lodge at Yosemite National Park. Some rooms overlook woodlands; the villas are roomy and come with kitchens. ✆ 901 W. Timber-line Dr • Map F1 • 407-824-3200 • www.disney world.com • $$$$

8 Disney's Port Orleans Resort

You can opt to stay in the French Quarter's colonial houses with iron balconies or in the Riverside's southern-style mansions. Gardeners love the landscaping, and shoppers like the location. ✆ 2201 Orleans Dr • Map F2 • 407-934-5000 • www. disneyworld.com • $$$

9 Hard Rock Hotel

Universal's second resort boasts Mission-style architecture and a rock 'n' roll theme. Rooms are attractive and comfortable; the best views are from those facing the lake. Guests get to skip the lines for rides and shows at Universal's parks. ✆ 5000 Universal Blvd • Map T1 • 407-503-7625 • www.universal orlando.com • $$$$

10 Disney's Value Resorts

The All-Star Movies, All-Star Music, and All-Star Sports resorts have relatively small rooms, but rates here are the cheapest in Walt Disney World Resort. ✆ 407-934-7639 • Map G1 • www.disney world.com • $$

Unless indicated, all hotels have DA, smoking rooms, A/C, pool, parking and kids' accommodation, and accept credit cards

Price Categories

For a standard, double room per night (with breakfast if included), taxes and extra charges.

$	under $90
$$	$90–180
$$$	$180–250
$$$$	over $250

Villas of Grand Cypress

🔟 Luxury Hotels

1 Hyatt Regency Grand Cypress

This vast resort is one of Orlando's most amazing places to stay. The 18-story atrium has inner and outer glass elevators with great views, some rooms have whirlpool baths, and the resort boasts a golf course, horseback riding, tennis courts (see p56), a beach, and plenty of nature, including a lake and waterfalls. ◈ 1 Grand Cypress Blvd • Map F2 • 407-239-1234 • www. grandcypress.hyatt.com • $$$$

2 Buena Vista Palace Resort

The classy rooms at this, the largest Lake Buena Vista hotel, have either balconies with lake views or patios. Hypo-allergenic evergreen rooms have air and water filter systems. The Top of the Palace bar offers free champagne to guests who go to enjoy the sunset. ◈ 1900 Buena Vista Dr • Map G2 • 407-827-2727 • www.buena vistapalace.com • $$$

3 Villas of Grand Cypress

The Hyatt's sister property offers condos and town houses, plus some suites. Some accommodations have Roman tubs and patios. Amenities include a golf course, tennis courts, and an equestrian center (see p56). ◈ 1 N. Jacaranda • Map F2 • 800-835-7377 • www.grand cypress.com • $$$$

4 Gaylord Palms Resort

Located on acres of beautiful gardens, this resort hosts five restaurants, two pools, two bars and three separate Florida-style residences. There's a full-service spa and childcare center, and it's well located for theme parks. ◈ 6000 W. Osceola Pkwy • Map G2 • 407-586-2000 • www.gaylord hotels.com • $$$

5 Renaissance Orlando Resort

Both the amenity-filled rooms and their marble bathrooms in this snazzy hotel are massive. Even the atrium, filled with aquariums, waterfalls, and palm trees, is 10 stories high. ◈ 6677 Sea Harbor Dr • Map T5 • 407-351-5555 • www.renaissancehotels. com • $$$$

6 Peabody Orlando

This hotel boasts an elegant feel, friendly staff, and a great location for I-Drive attractions. Home of the Peabody Ducks (see p46), it has four rooftop tennis courts, as well as a health center. ◈ 9801 International Dr • Map T4 • 407-352-4000 • www.peabody-orlando. com • $$$$

7 Marriott's Orlando World Center

The 2,000 rooms at this 28-story tower tend to be a bit smaller than others in this price category, but they come with plenty of in-room features. The resort boasts a wide array of facilities including a spa and the biggest pool in town. ◈ 8701 World Center Dr • Map G2 • 407-239-4200 • www. marriott-hotels.com • $$$

8 Grand Bohemian

Soft-as-clouds beds are one of this elegant downtown hotel's greatest selling points. Rooms are modern, and public areas display rare artworks. ◈ 325 S. Orange Ave • Map P3 • 407-313-9000 • www.grandbohe mianhotel.com • $$$$

9 Staybridge Suites Lake Buena Vista

The friendly staff and size of the suites make this an attractive choice for those who want to be near to, but not in, the clutches of Mickey. Rates include continental breakfast, and all suites have kitchens. ◈ 8751 Suitside Dr • Map F2 • 407-238-0777 • www. summerfield-orlando.com • $$$

10 Disney's Animal Kingdom Lodge

This Disney resort resembles a South African game lodge in a semi-circular kraal (compound). Rooms have an African theme and some have views of a wildlife-filled tropical savanna. ◈ 2901 Osceola Pkwy • Map G1 • 407-938-3000 • www.disneyworld. com • $$$$

Left **Doubletree Guest Suites** Right **Holiday Inn Walt Disney**

Mid-Price Hotels (A-G)

1 Best Western Lake Buena Vista Hotel

All rooms have balconies at this official Disney hotel, some of which overlook beautiful gardens bordering the lake. There's free transportation to Disney's major parks, and it's within walking distance of Marketplace, Pleasure Island, and West Side. ✪ *2000 Hotel Plaza Blvd • Map F2 • 407-828-2424 • www.downtowndisney hotels.com • $$*

2 Caribbean Beach Resort

Disney's largest hotel (with 2,112 rooms) is split into five "villages": Aruba, Trinidad, Martinique, Barbados, and Jamaica, each with its own pool and sandy beach. The rooms are on the small side but are good value. ✪ *900 Cayman Way • Map G2 • 407-934-3400 • www. disneyworld.com • $$$*

3 Celebration Hotel

The elegant lakefront rooms at this three-story, timber-framed resort offer a tranquil water-and-woodlands view. Facilities include an outdoor pool with Jacuzzi, a fitness center, and nature trails. There's an 18-hole golf course *(see p54)* too. ✪ *700 Bloom St • Map G2 • 407-566-6000 • www. celebrationhotel.com • $$$*

4 Courtyard at Lake Lucerne

Downtown's best B&B has four period buildings, from the Victorian Norment-Parry Inn to the Art Deco Wellborn House, which has apartments and a honeymoon suite. ✪ *211 N. Lucerne Circle E • Map P3 • 407-648-5188 • www. orlandohistoricinn.com • No pool • $$*

5 Courtyard by Marriott, Lake Buena Vista Centre

This mid-priced hotel has two outdoor heated swimming pools, a games room, and a Pizza Hut restaurant on site. It is well located for theme parks. ✪ *8501 Palm Pkwy • Map G2 • 407-239-6900 • www.courtyard.com • $$*

6 Extended Stay Deluxe Orlando Convention Center

Some of the 137 suites have wheelchair access, others are tailored to the hearing impaired. There's a heated pool, barbecues, and a Jacuzzi, and it's on the I-Ride Trolley circuit and provides a free shuttle to Disney. ✪ *8750 Universal Blvd • Map E3 • 407-903-1500 • www. extendedstay.com • $$*

7 Doubletree-Castle Resort

The towering spires of this themed hotel make it look like a fairytale castle – if castles came in pink and blue, that is. Its 216 rooms and seven suites come with big-screen TVs and Sony Playstations. The resort has a roof terrace, a fitness center, and two restaurants. ✪ *8629 International Dr • Map T2 • 407-345-1511 • www.doubletree hotels.com • $$*

8 Doubletree Guest Suites

After being welcomed with home-made cookies, head to your cozy one- or two-bedroomed suite at this official Disney hotel. With a landscaped pool and a spa, you can't fail to relax. ✪ *2305 Hotel Plaza Blvd • Map F2 • 407-934-1000 • www.double treeguestsuites.com • $$*

9 Doubletree Universal Orlando

A $16 million renovation helped convert this former convention hotel into one that woos travelers who want to be near the Universal parks. The hotel's two towers house 742 modern rooms and suites; those on the west side overlook the parks and CityWalk. ✪ *5780 Major Blvd • Map T2 • 407-351-1000 • www.hilton.com • $$*

10 Eó Inn

The best boutique hotel in town offers minimalist elegance with a personal touch. All rooms come with office facilities, and some overlook Lake Eola. Try the on-site spa *(see p59)* if in need of pampering. ✪ *227 N. Eola Dr • Map N3 • 407-481-8485 • www.eoinn.com • No pool • No smoking rooms • $$$*

Unless indicated, all hotels have DA, smoking rooms, A/C, pool, parking and kids' accommodation, and accept credit cards.

Price Categories

For a standard, double room per night (with breakfast if included), taxes and extra charges.	
$	under $90
$$	$90–180
$$$	$180–250
$$$$	over $250

Nickelodeon Family Suites by Holiday Inn

⑩ Mid-Price Hotels (H–Z)

1 Nickelodeon Family Suites by Holiday Inn
Children rule in this resort, which has Kidsuites (sleeping up to seven) with big-screen TVs. Other types of suite include Cinemasuites, with even bigger TVs. Activities offered range from karaoke to ping-pong, and there are also two water parks. ◎ 14500 Continental Gateway • Map G3 • 877-387-5437 • www.hifamily suites.com • $$$

2 Holiday Inn Sunspree Resort
If keeping the kids happy is top priority, this hotel is a good bet. Apart from the themed, two-roomed Kidsuites (space ship, tree house, igloo, and so on), there's a free activities program for 3–12-year-olds. Children even have their own restaurant. ◎ 13351 Apopka-Vineland Rd • Map G3 • 407-239-4500 • www.kidsuites.com • $$

3 Holiday Inn Walt Disney
This comfortable hotel makes for a good choice on the Hotel Plaza strip. All the well-appointed rooms have Nintendos, and the glass elevator that scales the 14-story, plant-filled atrium makes for a more exciting ride than most. There's a free Disney shuttle. ◎ 1805 Hotel Plaza Blvd • Map F2 • 407-828-8888 • www. hiorlando.com • $$

4 Quality Suites Orlando
These modern luxury suites in neutral tones, with spacious living rooms and kitchens, can sleep up to six. Free hors d'oeuvres, beer, and wine are served early evening in the lobby (Mon–Thu). Rates include breakfast. ◎ 8200 Palm Pkwy • Map F2 • 407-465-8200 • www.qualitysuites lvb.com • No DA • $$

5 Hotel Royal Plaza
Some of the spacious rooms at this hotel have whirlpools; pool-side ones have balconies or patios. The pool is heated, and there's a Jacuzzi, spa, fitness center, and four lit tennis courts. ◎ 1905 Hotel Plaza Blvd • Map F2 • 407-828-2828 • www. downtowndisneyhotels.com • $$$

6 Radisson World Gate
Don't expect the normal Renaissance high standard, since the 577 rooms at this hotel are more motel-like. Still, price, location, and service make it attractive. ◎ 3011 Maingate Lane • Map G2 • 407-396-1400 • www.radissonworldgate. com • $

7 Heron Cay Lakeview B&B
This Victorian-style hotel situated within a large garden overlooks Lake Dora. The Queen Victoria suite, with its crimson furnishings and four-poster bed, is the most inviting of the six rooms. Gourmet breakfasts can include spinach strata and potato pancakes. ◎ 495 Old Hwy 441 • Off map • 352-383-4050 • $$$

8 Springhill Suites
This pleasant suite hotel located in the Marriott Village is close to Disney. All the suites have a king-size or two double beds, plus separate living and cooking areas. ◎ 8623 Vineland Ave • Map G2 • 407-938-9001 • www. springhillsuites.com • $–$$

9 Thurston House
Built in 1885, and set in woodland, this charming B&B offers a quiet retreat, popular with adults. The four rooms, with queen-size beds, overlook Lake Eulalia. It's smoke-free and has no pool, but the home-away-from-home atmosphere is a winner. ◎ 851 Lake Ave • Map F3 • 407-539-1911 • www. thurstonhouse.com • No DA • $$

10 Liki Tiki Village
Just 7 miles (11 km) from the south gate of Disney, Liki Tiki is a luxurious complex offering furnished condos. With a vast water park on site, the kids may never leave for the parks. ◎ 17777 Bali Blvd, Winter Garden • Map G1 • 407-856-7190 • www.likitiki.com • $$

Left **Best Value Hawaiian Inn** Right **Quality Inn sign**

Inexpensive Hotels (A-H)

1 Best Western Mount Vernon Inn

Located some 20 miles (32 km) north of Disney World, this is a cozy, colonial-style motel, with friendly staff. There's a city park across the street and many of Downtown's attractions are nearby. ✆ 110 S. Orlando Ave • Map H4 • 407-647-1166 • www. bestwestern.com • $

2 Comfort Inn Lake Buena Vista

Well located to the theme parks, this hotel offers a free shuttle service. There are two swimming pools and a mini-market deli for buying snacks. Breakfast is included and kids stay and eat for free at the on-site restaurant. ✆ 8442 Palm Pkwy • Map F3 • 407-996-7300 • www. comfortinnorlando.com • $

3 Howard Johnson Inn Maingate East

Rooms at this inn are sparse and small, but they do come with Nintendo consoles. Ask for a room at the rear to escape the noise of traffic. One child eats free with each paying adult in the restaurant. Efficiencies (small serviced apartments) are available. ✆ 6051 W. Irlo Bronson Memorial Hwy • Map G2 • 407-396-1748 • www. hojomge.com • $

4 Best Value Hawaiian Inn

The rooms at this Hawaiian-themed hotel (suited to families on a budget) are small, but some sleep five. The location – on Disney's doorstep – and affordability are a winning mix, but there's no elevator to get to upper-story rooms. ✆ 7514 W. Irlo Bronson Hwy • Map G1 • 407-396-2000 • www. bestvalue.com • $

5 Days Inn Orlando Lakeside

Cheap rates and a good location at the northern end of I-Drive are the selling points for this Days Inn. The rooms are small and basic; some have a lake view. ✆ 7335 Sand Lake Rd • Map S3 • 407-351-1900 • www. daysinn.com • $

6 Days Inn Convention Center North of SeaWorld

This branch of the Days Inn chain makes a good base for convention-goers and vacationers alike. The hotel is surrounded by landscaped grounds and has a pancake restaurant and playground. ✆ 9990 International Dr • Map T5 • 407-352-8700 • www.days inn.com • $

7 Best Western Lakeside

Located just 2 miles (1km) from Disneyworld, the hotel offers a free shuttle service to many theme parks. There are also three restaurants and three pools within its 24 landscaped acres. Rooms are bright and spacious, offering good value for money. ✆ 7769 W. Highway 192 • Map G2 • 407-396-2222 • www. bestwestern.com • $

8 Clarion Resort & Water Park

This three-story motel has moderate-sized rooms and is a good base if you're into sport and nature, with facilities and activities close by. In the restaurant, children under 10 eat free if accompanied by paying adults. ✆ 2261 E. Irlo Bronson Memorial Hwy • Map H5 • 407-846-2221 • www.choicehotels.com • $$

9 Galleria Palms Hotel & Suites

This hotel has a newer and nicer feel than most establishments in this price bracket. Rooms are smallish but sleep up to four. There's a free Disney shuttle, and rates include breakfast, free internet access, and free local phone calls. ✆ 3000 Maingate Lane • Map G2 • 407-396-6300 • www.galleriapalms orlando.com • $$

10 Home Sweet Home Eastgate

The rather basic rooms – as in most cheap chains – are small, but this five-story motel has a video games room, a playground, two tennis courts, and is not far from Disney. ✆ 5565 W. Irlo Bronson Memorial Hwy • Map G2 • 407-396-0707 • $

Unless indicated, all hotels have DA, smoking rooms, A/C, pool, parking and kids' accommodation, and accept credit cards.

Price Categories

For a standard, double room per night (with breakfast if included), taxes and extra charges.

$	under $90
$$	$90–180
$$$	$180–250
$$$$	over $250

Left **Best Western Mount Vernon Inn**

🔟 Inexpensive Hotels (I–Z)

Inn Nova
The motel-style rooms (with two double beds) are on the small side at the Inn Nova, but the location, just west of Disney, is a plus. Breakfast is included. ✆ *9330 W. Irlo Bronson Memorial Hwy • Map G3 • 863-424-8420 • No smoking rooms • $*

Metropolitan Express
Just one mile (1.6 km) from the Wet 'n Wild and Universal parks, this motel offers free transport to Disney. Its rooms – with two double beds – are no-frills but pleasant. Rates include breakfast. ✆ *6323 International Dr • Map T2 • 407-351-4430 or 800-276-7415 • www.enjoyflorida hotels.com • $*

International Drive Travelodge
The Travelodge is a good choice for value-conscious guests who want to be in the heart of I-Drive's attractions. It's more upscale than some in this category and has a great tropical pool bar. ✆ *5859 American Way • Map T2 • 407-345-8880 • www.travelodge.com • $*

Park Inn
This budget option is a modern motel situated well away from the main tourist resorts. But its location is great for anyone interested in shopping as well as

more cultural diversions. Rates include continental breakfast. ✆ *951 Wymore Rd • Map B4 • 407-539-1955 • www.orlando parkinn.com • $*

Ramada Inn
The rooms are a step above most in this price category, and the majority are situated away from the noise of I-Drive traffic. The motel is located between SeaWorld and the Universal parks, and it's on the I-Ride Trolley circuit *(see p127)*. Rates include continental breakfast. ✆ *8342 Jamaican Ct • Map T3 • 407-363-1944 • www.ramada.com • $*

Quality Inn Plaza
This is a good-value hotel given its location on I-Drive, just opposite Pointe Orlando. The standard rooms are really quite small, so if space is an issue, opt for a semi-suite. Three pools, two games rooms, and a 24-hour deli are among the on-site amenities. ✆ *9000 International Dr • Map T4 • 407-996-8585 • www.qualityinn-orlando.com • $*

La Quinta Inn & Suites UCF
This hotel, near the University of Central Florida, is for guests who want an east Orlando location. Rooms are comfortable, and rates include breakfast, local phone calls, internet

access, and weekday newspapers. ✆ *11805 Research Pkwy • Off map • 407-737-6075 • www.laquinta.com • $$*

Ramada Inn Resort Eastgate
The Ramada's rooms have balconies, two double beds, and Nintendos. Kids 12 and under eat free with a paying adult. Facilities include basketball and tennis courts. ✆ *5150 W. Irlo Bronson Memorial Hwy • Map G3 • 407-396-1111 • www.ramada.com • $$*

Palms Hotel & Villas
This hotel is well located for Walt Disney World Resort and offers a complimentary shuttle service to the Disney theme parks. The Guest Services Desk will help get you tickets and reservations. There is a complimentary breakfast. ✆ *3100 Parkway Blvd • Map G2 • 407-396-8484 • www.palmshotelsand villas.com • $$*

Royal Celebration Inn
Situated on Lake Cecile, this motel is five miles (8 km) from Mickey's place. The rooms are a bit cramped, but they have Nintendos. The inn has a sandy lakeside beach, with jet skis and water-skiing on offer. ✆ *4944 W. Irlo Bronson Memorial Hwy • Map H3 • 407-396-4455 • www.wellesleyonline.com • $*

For ways to have fun on the cheap **See pp46–7**

Left **Sheraton's Vistana Resort** Right **Beach Tree Villas**

TOP 10 Condo & Timeshare Rentals

1 Disney Vacation Club

The same upscale Disney units that are sold as time-shares are also available for rental. Properties are located at the Old Key West Resort (white clap-board houses), Boardwalk Villas (see p142), and Wilderness Lodge (see p142). ✆ 800-800-9100 • Map F2, G2 & F1 • www. dvcresorts.com • $$$$

2 Sheraton's Vistana Resort

This resort offers modern one- and two-bedroom villas and town houses, packed with home com-forts, that can be rented by the week. The tennis facilities are excellent, with both clay and all-weather courts. ✆ 8800 Vistana Center Dr • Map G2 • 407-239-3100 • www. starwood.com/sheraton • $$$

3 Summer Bay Resort

Accommodation at Sum-mer Bay ranges from one-bedroom condos to three-bedroom villas; all have washers and dryers. The property has a clubhouse and offers a Friday-night luau (traditional Hawaiian meal). ✆ 17805 W. Irlo Bronson Memorial Hwy • Map G1 • 877-782-9387 • www.summerbayresort. com • $$

4 Endless Summer Vacation Homes

This organization leases two- to five-bedroom

houses in several loca-tions around Central Florida. All have their own pools; some are near golf links. You need to pay a premium for any stays of less than seven nights. ✆ 3501 W. Vine St, Suite 131, Kissimmee • 800-554-4378 • www. esvflorida.com • $$

5 Marriott Vacation Club International

Marriott's timeshare pro-gram covers five Orlando locations. The apartments and villas can also be rented by the week. Some of the villas have patios or porches, and facilities include activity programs, fitness centers, golf-course privileges, tennis courts, clubhouses, and saunas. ✆ 800-845-5279 • www. vacationclub.com • $$$

6 Holiday Villas

For generous living space (although bedrooms are on the small side), Holiday Villas offers two- and three-bedroom condos that can sleep up to eight. Each comes with a washer and dryer. ✆ 2928 Vineland Rd • Map G3 • 800-344-3959 • www. holidayvillas.com • $$

7 Blue Tree Resort

Blue Tree's elegant and spacious one- and two-bedroom villas are well-located for Disney attractions. The resort has four pools, two tennis courts, a volleyball court, and a playground.

Rates are available with or without housekeeping services. ✆ 12007 Cypress Run Rd • Map F3 • 407-238-6000 • www.bluetree resort.com • $$

8 Orlando Breeze Resort

Polo Park, with its two- and three-bedroom villas, is a real home-away-from-home. It lacks the crowds and tourist frenzy of the mainstream areas. ✆ 12727 Hwy 27 N. • Off map • 863-420-3838 • www.silverleafresorts.com • Smoke free • $$

9 Island One Resorts

There are four themed resorts to choose from, offering roomy one- to three-bedroom condos and villas. Facilities vary, but range from whirlpools to nature trails, and they sell discount attraction tickets. ✆ 2345 Sand Lake Rd, Suite 100 • 407-859-8900 • www.islandone. com • $$

10 Beach Tree Villas

Great for families, the Beach Tree has two- to five-bedroom homes, the larger of which have private pools. There's an on-site recreation center, sauna, and a tennis court, but rates don't include an extra cleaning fee. Villas have a four-night mini-mum stay; houses have a five-night minimum. ✆ 2545 Chatham Circle • Map G3 • 407-396-7416 • www.beachtreevillas.com • Smoke free • $$

Unless indicated, all hotels have DA, smoking rooms, A/C, pool, parking and kids' accommodation, and accept credit cards.

Price Categories

For a standard, double room per night (with breakfast if included), taxes and extra charges.

$	under $90
$$	$90–180
$$$	$180–250
$$$$	over $250

Left **Fort Summit Orlando KOA Kampground**

⑩ Close to Nature

① Fort Wilderness Resort & Campground

Vast tracts of cypress and pine trees, fish-filled lakes, and fresh air envelop this Disney resort. It has 783 tent sites plus 409 cabins, which sleep up to six and have kitchens (the newer ones also have sun decks). Canoeing and horseback riding are two of the many outdoor activities on offer. ◎ 4510 N. Fort Wilderness Trail • Map F1 • 407-824-2900 • www.disneyworld.com • $

② Disney's Saratoga Springs Resort & Spa

Choose from one-bedroom bungalows, two-bedroom town houses, fairway villas next to Disney golf courses, or three-bedroom Treehouse Villas 10 ft (3 m) off the ground. Most include daily housekeeping and there are lots of recreation choices. ◎ 1960 Magnolia Way • 407-827-1100 • www.disneyworld.com • $$$$

③ Southport Park Campground & Marina

This relaxing park is in 25-acres (10 ha) of lakeside woods. While away time on site by fishing, wandering among the wildlife (such as eagles and deer), or by taking an airboat trip. There are RV and tent sites with full hook-ups. ◎ 2001 W. Southport Rd • 407-933-5822 • www.southportpark.com • $

④ Floridian RV Resort

This woodsy retreat near Lake Tohopekaliga offers full hook-ups for RVs, two clubhouses, a playground, tennis courts, and a volley-ball court. There are plenty of leisure activities in the area, such as airboat rides and parasailing. ◎ 5150 Boggy Creek Rd • Off map • 407-892-5171 • www.florida-rv-parks.com • $

⑤ Orlando SW/Fort Summit KOA

A great place to camp if you want to be close to Walt Disney World and SeaWorld.There are RV sites, camp sites, and cabins. RV sites can have cable TV and modem dataport connected for an extra charge. ◎ PO Box 22182, Lake Buena Vista • 888-562-4712 • www.koa.com/where/fl/09327.htm • $

⑥ Clerbrook Golf & RV Resort

This large site, popular with golfers, offers 1,250 RV hook-ups, non-smoking villas, as well as amenities including a driving range, four whirlpools, a library, and a beauty salon. ◎ 20005 Hwy 27 • Off map • 352-394-5513 • www.florida-rv-parks.com • $

⑦ Cypress Cove Nudist Resort

Unself-conscious couples and families, with either American Association for Nude Recreation or Cypress Cove resort membership, stay in villas, rooms, and RV sites here. ◎ 4425 Pleasant Hill Rd • Off map • 407-933-5870 • www.suncove.com • $$

⑧ Fort Summit Orlando KOA Kampground

This resort offers full hook-ups for RVs, as well as small timber cabins and pitches for tents. There's a store, laundromats, and internet access. ◎ 2525 Frontage Rd • Off map • 863-424-1880 • www.fortsummit.com • $

⑨ Circle F. Dude Ranch Camp

This kids' summer camp is also a family retreat on selected weekends between November and May. Hay rides, horseback riding, lake swimming, and sailing are some of the activities on offer. Weekend rates include five meals. ◎ Hwy 60 & Dude Ranch Rd • Off map • 863-676-4113 • www.circle-f-duderanch.com • smoke-free • No DA • $$$$

⑩ Orlando Winter Garden RV Resort

Pines and ponds are all around this RV resort, about a 30-minute drive from Disney World. It boasts lots of facilities such as laundry, games room, dances, bingo, and barbecues. Popular with an older crowd. ◎ 13905 W. Colonial Dr • Map C1 • 407-656-1415 • www.florida-rv-parks.com • $

General Index

Index

Acknowledgements

The Authors
Richard Grula lives in Orlando and specializes in writing about the downtown and cultural scenes. He's contributed to the *Orlando Weekly*, *Orlando Magazine*, Sidewalk.com, and *Time Out's Guide to Miami and Orlando*.

Jim and Cynthia Tunstall are Central Florida natives who have written five other Florida guides, including Frommer's *Walt Disney World & Orlando*.

Produced by Departure Lounge, London
Editorial Director Naomi Peck
Art Editor Lee Redmond
Editor Clare Tomlinson
Designer Lisa Kosky, Rachel Symons
DTP Designer Ingrid Vienings
Picture Researcher Monica Allende, Ellen Root
Research Assistance Amaia Allende, Ana Virginia Aranha, Diveen Henry, Faiyaz Kara
Proofreader Stephanie Driver
Indexer Hilary Bird
Fact Checkers Phyllis and Arvin Steinberg
Photographers Gregory Matthews, Magnus Rew
Additional Photography Demetrio Carrasco, Stephen Whitehorn, Linda Whitwham,
Illustrator Lee Redmond
Maps John Plumer

AT DORLING KINDERSLEY
Publishing Manager Kate Poole
Senior Art Editor Marisa Renzullo
Director of Publishing Gillian Allan
Publisher Douglas Amrine
Revisions Co-ordinators Claire Baranowski, Rada Radojicic, Mani Ramaswamy, Ros Walford
Assistant Revisions Co-ordinators Emma Anacootee, Sherry Collins, Laura Jones, Mary Ormandy
Revisions Fact Checker Marian Virginia Warder
Revisions Designer Susana Smith
Revisions Editor Esther Labi, Kathryn Lane
Cartography Co-ordinator Casper Morris
DTP Jason Little, Conrad van Dyk
Production Sarah Dodd

Picture Credits
Placement Key: t-top; tc-top centre; tr-top right; cla-centre left above; ca-centre above; cra-centre right above; cl-centre left; c-centre; cr-centre right; clb-centre left below; cb-centre below; crb-centre right below; bl-below left; bc-below centre; br-below right.

The publishers would like to thank the following individuals, companies and picture libraries for permission to reproduce their photographs:

ALAMY IMAGES: Gerrit de Heus 27cl; Ilene MacDonald 66tl, ARABIAN NIGHTS: 80b; THE BLACK OLIVE: 117tl; BLUE MARTINI 74tl, BOGGY CREEK AIRBOAT RIDES: 110tl

CHRIS CASLER: 77ca, 78tl, 78b; 2000 CORNELL FINE ARTS MUSEUM: 118tr CORBIS /Kevin Morris 64tr; /David Muench 36-7; /Patrick Ward 109bl

DEPARTURE LOUNGE: 136tr, 137tl; DISCOVERY COVE: 48tr, 50–51, 97c;

© DISNEY ENTERPRISES, INC: 1c; 8–9, 10, 12–13, 14, 16–17, 18–19, 89, 91, 92, 93, 94, 95, back jacket r; DOUBLETREE GUEST SUITES: 144tl; FLORIDA ECO-SAFARIS: 108bl, FLORIDA FILM FESTIVAL 64c, 65br; GENESIS SPACE PHOTO LIBRARY: 40tc, 40c

HARD ROCK Orlando: 76cl; © HEIDI TARGEE: 46tl, 99c, 114b; HOLIDAY INN: 141tl; HOLIDAY INN WALT DISNEY: 144tr; ICEBAR Orlando: 100tl

KENNEDY SPACE CENTER: 3br, 7b, 38–39c, 38c, 38b, 39t, 39c, 39b, 40tl; KISSIMMEE-ST CLOUD CONVENTION & VISITORS' BUREAU, 48c, 108tc, 110tr; Doug Dukane: 47, 56tl, 56tr, 57tr, 106tl, 109tl, 110tc

© MEDIEVAL TIMES: 80tl; MERRITT ISLAND NATIONAL WILDLIFE REFUGE: 7cr, 36c, 36, 37b

© NASA: 40tr, 41c, 41b; ORLANDO TOURISM BUREAU, London: 53, 57cl, 57cr, 60tl, 60tr

ORLANDO & ORANGE COUNTY CONVENTION & VISITORS' BUREAU, INC: 3tr, 44tl, 54b, 55, 62tl, 62tr, 62b, 63, 67tl, 75tr, 76cl,101tr, 106tr, 109tr, 109br, 112c, 115cr, 119t, 127tl; ORLANDO INTERNATIONAL FRINGE FESTIVAL: 64tl; ORLANDO-UCF SHAKESPEARE FESTIVAL: 65bl RIVERSHIP ROMANCE: Jeff Drake 84cr

SEAWORLD ORLANDO, FLORIDA All rights reserved: 3bl, 3tl, 7tr, 28–29c, 28t, 28c, 29t, 29clb; 30tl, 30tr, 30b, 31c, 31b, 32–33, 42–43b, 43t, 43c, 129, 139tl, Jason Collier 29clb; SKYVENTURE LLC, ORLANDO: 45tc; THE SOCIAL CLUB: 116tl; SPA AT THE WYNDHAM PALACE RESORT: 59; STARWOOD 148tl

© UNIVERSAL ORLANDO: 3tc, 4–5, 6tr, 6bl, 20–21c, 20t, 20c, 20b, 21t, 22tl, 22tc, 22tr, 22c, 23c, 23b, 24–25, 24t, 24c, 24b, 25t, 26t, 26tr, 42tl, 42tr, 42c, 43b, 46tr, 65cr, 68b, 86–87, 96tr, 97t, 104tl, 126tr, 142; US FISH AND WILDLIFE SERVICE: Gary M. Stolz 37t; VILLAS OF GRAND CYPRESS: 56t, 56c, 57br, 88tr, 143; WALT DISNEY WORLD DOLPHIN RESORT: 69tl; WET 'N WILD: 7cl, 34–35c, 34t, 34cl, 34b, 35t, 35cr, 35b, 48tl, 96tl

© ZORA NEALE HURSTON NATIONAL MUSEUM OF FINE ARTS *Festival Girl*, Jane Turner 121cl

Front Flap: SEAWORLD PHOTO/VIDEO SERVICES, FLORIDA: bcl

All other images are © Dorling Kindersley. For further information see www.dkimages.com.

Index of Main Streets

Street Index